# THE AI LEADER

# THE AI LEADER
## MASTERY OF HUMANS AND MACHINES IN THE WORKPLACE

J. MARK MUNOZ
AL NAQVI

FIRST HILL BOOKS
An imprint of Wimbledon Publishing Company Limited (WPC)

This edition first published in UK and USA 2021
by FIRST HILL BOOKS
75–76 Blackfriars Road, London SE1 8HA, UK
or PO Box 9779, London SW19 7ZG, UK
and
244 Madison Ave #116, New York, NY 10016, USA

Copyright © J. Mark Munoz and Al Naqvi 2021

The author asserts the moral right to be identified as the author of this work.

All rights reserved. Without limiting the rights under copyright reserved above, no part of this publication may be reproduced, stored or introduced into a retrieval system, or transmitted, in any form or by any means (electronic, mechanical, photocopying, recording or otherwise), without the prior written permission of both the copyright owner and the above publisher of this book.

*British Library Cataloguing-in-Publication Data*
A catalogue record for this book is available from the British Library.

Library of Congress Control Number: 2021941615

ISBN-13: 978-1-78527-993-5 (Hbk)
ISBN-10: 1-78527-993-9 (Hbk)

This title is also available as an e-book.

*To Kulsoom Naqvi, my mother and the first example of great leadership in my life*

*Al (Ali) Naqvi*

*To my parents Edgar and Charity, who inspired me to be a leader in their own unique way*

*J. Mark Munoz*

# CONTENTS

| | | |
|---|---|---|
| CHAPTER 1 | Why AI Leadership? | 1 |
| CHAPTER 2 | Intelligence Comes Alive | 17 |
| CHAPTER 3 | A Leader Who Tames Machines | 33 |
| CHAPTER 4 | The Three States of an AI Leader | 47 |
| CHAPTER 5 | State 1 Leadership: Business Context | 61 |
| CHAPTER 6 | State 2 Leadership: Strategic Ownership | 71 |
| CHAPTER 7 | State 3 Leadership: Stakeholder Responsibility | 83 |
| CHAPTER 8 | AI Leadership and the Way Forward | 103 |
| *References* | | 145 |
| *Index* | | 151 |

CHAPTER 1

# WHY AI LEADERSHIP?

*The range of what we think and do is limited by what we fail to notice. And because we fail to notice that we fail to notice, there is little we can do to change; until we notice how failing to notice shapes our thoughts and deeds.*
—R. D. LAING

### EXECUTIVE INTERVIEW 1

### Jeff Adams, CEO, Cobalt Speech and Language

Authors: How would you describe the current state of artificial intelligence (AI) in your industry? In what way has AI transformed your organization?

*Adams: Since "my industry" is the AI software industry, these are hard questions for me to answer. However, let me step back and comment on what I see as the broader picture. It feels to me as if many business leaders have gotten the message that they need to embrace AI or be left behind. At the same time, they don't really understand why they need AI, or where it might fit within their organization, services, and processes, and so they are stumbling around, casting about for a token AI application to make them feel better, and ease their fears of being left behind. Much of the time, this ends up taking the form of an AI-informed tool to help them analyze customers and sales. However, without appropriate training and deep knowledge on the part of the employees using this tool, it ends up being not much more beneficial than a spreadsheet.*

*What business really need to do is to get some training to change the way they think about their processes. AI is not a "trick." It is a way of using empirical data to inform everything you do, from manufacturing, to logistics and supply chain processes, to product definition, to customer tracking, and beyond. A simple app will not take care of this for you. Businesses should hire AI companies to partner with them at every level. They should hire senior staff* that have credible training in AI. Despite the scrambling to latch onto a token AI solution and implement it, many companies will still find themselves left behind.

Our company (Cobalt Speech and Language) focuses on that particular corner of the AI world having to do with human language—understanding speech, analyzing written language, building conversational interfaces and applications, and learning about people from the way they speak. For the rest of my responses here, I'll direct my comments specifically to this "human/computer language interaction" facet of AI.

Authors: What is not being done right in the AI revolution?

*Adams:* There are a few sins being committed by those of us working on speech and language. Perhaps the biggest offense is that most commercial speech and language tech providers (including Cobalt) are focusing first on the most commercially viable languages. Language technology requires a substantial amount of effort for each language supported, to train the software on the particular sounds, words, constructs, and meanings of a language. Of necessity, most companies start out with a focus on English, which represents fewer than 5 percent of the world's speakers. The next languages to be added are typically the dominant European and American languages: German, French, Italian, and Spanish. Collectively known as "EFIGS", supporting these five languages requires roughly five times as much effort as English alone and still only covers the native languages of roughly 13 percent of the world's speakers.

Perhaps the company that has invested the most in language coverage is Google. They support (to some degree) speech technology for more than a hundred languages and dialects, covering over 60 percent of the world's speakers, but even with this Herculean effort, more than a third of the world's speakers have no access to language technology. That includes speakers of some of the most widely spoken languages of Asia (including India), Africa, and the Pacific.

Authors: Where do you think opportunities exist with regard to AI in the workplace?

*Adams:* There are vast opportunities to include speech and language technology in the workplace, many of which are rarely considered. Of course, there is the opportunity to automate many processes by giving them voice interfaces. We have worked with partners to give voice interfaces to factory workers, surgeons, pilots, call center agents, and hospitality workers, and there are many, many opportunities to extend that to other fields.

We are also beginning to see an increase in use of automated systems to support employees. Employees might be able to take care of tasks with a phone call such as requesting leave, getting information on employee benefits, and filing applications for leave.

There are also opportunities for a more passive use of speech and language technology, as a means of watching out for employees' well-being and improve performance. Operators of heavy machinery (including long-distance drivers, pilots, and construction workers, for example) might have their routine speech monitored to detect signs of fatigue, to recommend appropriate times to take a break and refresh. Employees who deal with customers on a regular basis (either over the phone, by e-mail/chat, or in person) might be monitored to make sure they are treating customers well and giving correct information. In certain cases, an employee might monitor another employee's speech to detect signs of disease or impairment. These passive use cases are currently largely ignored when considering speech and language applications.

Authors: In your opinion, what should and what should not be automated? Why?

*Adams*: Automation should lift employees' spirit and morale. It should contribute to their well-being and free them from menial, degrading tasks. When asking what should be automated, managers should think about whether a task can be done accurately and effectively via automation, whether employees will be empowered by it, and the cost/benefit comparison of the particular automation.

Voice needs increasingly to be part of the picture. Employees are increasingly accustomed to interacting with devices and processes by voice, and most people are quite comfortable with that, especially younger workers. Outdated data entry processes need to be replaced by more natural voice interfaces. We've seen examples in industry where archaic control processes that took years to learn are being replaced by simple voice interfaces, allowing employers access to a larger, younger workforce.

Authors: How should companies prioritize AI projects? How are you doing it?

*Adams*: Fundamentally, there is nothing special about "AI." It simply reflects a modern, data-driven approach to analysis, decision-making, and productivity. There should not be projects that are "AI" and others that are not "AI". Everything should be informed by AI, and companies should embrace data-driven efficiencies in every situation.

Authors: Companies are part of an economic ecosystem including various stakeholders such as other companies, government, academia, and others. What role do stakeholders need to play to help AI flourish in companies?

*Adams*: Everyone has a role to play. Academia need to begin training a new workforce to think in terms of empirical data-driven decision-making. Governments need to support

> *companies and universities through grants, scholarships, and appropriate contract work. Companies that are hiring need to make it clear to students that familiarity with AI principles is an important and universal prerequisite in today's job market.*
>
> Authors: What do you think is the future of AI in the workplace? How will work be transformed?
>
> *Adams: AI will win out in the long run. Companies that embrace AI will slowly win out over those that don't, and within a decade or two, the questions we are asking today will sound as quaint as, "should companies embrace electricity?" Work will be transformed in subtle ways that we can't really predict today, simply because we always see the future "through a glass, darkly."*

What is AI leadership and why should you care about it? This is a question that you may not have considered before. You may have worn the hat of being a leader or held a leadership title such as director, vice president, or C-suite title. But a world undergoing a dramatic technological shift changes many other things aside from just technology. It changes leaders. It creates new types of leaders with different set of qualities. As the AI revolution unfolds, it requires a new type of leader that is attuned to the times.

To stay competitive today, you must have a roadmap for intelligent automation. The issue is that you can automate quickly, but irresponsible automation is a recipe for failure. Irresponsible automation can destroy your company and can negatively impact human civilization, economy, institutions, and the planet. As Boeing discovered after losing two passenger planes, which led to hundreds of deaths, a new level of responsibility is needed for autonomous and intelligent technologies. What every company needs, what every government agency needs, and what every nonprofit needs, is responsible intelligent automation.

We are experiencing a massive shift in the economic and social structures in our world. This structural shift is not driven by the industrial-era mechanical machines or information-age computer programming and Internet connectivity. Instead, it is being shaped by intelligent automation. Intelligent automation is when machines of all forms—mechanical and digital—perform work intelligently. This means they learn to perform tasks that typically require human intelligence. In some ways all that had happened in the previous industrial history of humankind is being redone—almost analogous to a body getting a working brain. This technological shift has the potential to produce a powerful change in how we work, what we do, how we relate, and how we live. As every product and service known to mankind—and the supporting infrastructure to develop, manufacture or deliver such services and products—are being transformed to an intelligent status, corporate executives and leaders are confused. On one end, they want to stay competitive and drive innovation. On the other end, this change appears to be too complex and almost counter intuitive. Experts from fields typically removed from traditional corporate environments (e.g., neuroscience, mathematics, cognitive science, AI) are leading this revolution. Leaders from both business side and traditional IT stand on the sidelines, unprepared and lost about how to understand and embrace the massive influx of new capabilities.

The real question is that how to lead organizations composed of both humans and intelligent digital workers? We contend that a different type of leader is needed to lead this revolution—one who

- focuses on creating new business value from intelligent automation.
- commits to a far deeper and different ethics model.
- develops a new sense of self-awareness.

This book will not turn you into a machine learning expert, but it will help you become a leader of a firm that wants to become an AI-centric company. The target audience for this book are all the executives—regardless of their background—who want to develop an understanding of how to lead in the new era of AI. The ground rules have changed, but they are not what you think. The fundamental attribute to become an effective leader for the AI is *responsibility*. Responsibility to this world, to your businesses, to our governments, to humans, to our future generations, and to the environment will determine if intelligent automation will create a world we can all be proud of or lead to the dystopia many associate with AI. Experts are concerned that automation achieved without *responsibility* will lead to massive destruction and can even wipe out the entire human civilization.

Yet our attitude toward automation and responsibility continues to be cavalier.

In the excitement to create wealth and fame, most universities and training programs have taken a singular view to teach executives about the merits of intelligent automation. We believe it is critical to tie automation with responsibility—an integral part of AI leadership. True AI leadership means producing powerful business results with intelligent automation while staying responsible. An AI leader needs to create value with intelligent automation and do it responsibly.

## AUTOMATION HAS A COST AND AI WILL MAKE IT WORSE

They knew how to hold large gatherings, but this event was remarkably different. The staff of the lavish New York City Fifth Avenue Hotel was anxious to make sure that everything would go perfectly. On a summer day in 2015, history was about to be made. Covered with a blue carpet, a massive platform was prepared for the distinguished event. American flags were neatly lined up in the back of the stage. A podium was placed right in the middle. Behind this podium, Donald Trump would stand and deliver his speech to become a candidate for the US presidency. The opulent setting of the magnificent room provided plenty of seating and additional space on the second floor for people to listen to the announcement. Moments before the announcement, amid flashing lights of cameras and cheering crowds, Donald Trump and his wife came down the golden escalator and it became the iconic scene that was played repeatedly by the media during and after the election cycle. When Trump made his announcement to run for the president of the United States, few people took him as a serious contender. Donald Trump, the real estate mogul, the reality television star, the playboy—what chance did he have to assume the greatest position on the face of the earth or to even qualify as the nominee, many asked. With smirks on their faces, political pundits and journalists rejected Donald Trump as a realistic option. He was viewed as a fleeting fad that will fade away as soon as America gets serious about its choices. Viewed by many as a popularity-seeking stunt, much like Stephen Colbert's run for presidency in 2012, experts gave Donald Trump few months of showbiz fame.

But the inconceivable happened. Trump began pocketing state after state as his competitors fell off the race board one by one. The smirks of pundits turned into headshakes of disbelief, and at times even rage, as Donald Trump soared to become the Republican nominee and then the president of the United States of America.

In the previous two election cycles, statisticians and data scientists had accurately predicted President Obama's victory. Equipped with powerful computers with massive data processing capabilities, the data scientists churned billions of pieces of information to understand and predict voter preferences. With a high degree of confidence, they predicted the election of President Obama—and their predictions came true. At that time, big data was being viewed as the answer to such problems. It was claimed that the uncertainty inherent in the elections was now removed. From observing things as simple as purchasing behaviors and travel habits, computers were used to understand and predict voter behavior. But when it came to Donald Trump, these oracles of voter behavior surprised their human masters. The data machines designed to spew out the political landscapes gave a completely different and misleading picture. The smart agents, scouts of information collection, that penetrated the depths of our consciousness and invaded the privacies of our opinions brought back bad information that led many to see Donald Trump as a vagary of political disposition, a quirk in the otherwise mature and steady voter temperament. They turned out to be wrong. As the pundits found out, Donald Trump was not a flyby phenomenon. What was at work was not just a passive voter profiling technology to prepare lists for canvassing but instead an active, forward deployed network of intelligent bots that knew how to inspire the base beyond anyone's wildest dreams. AI had been unleashed and America gulped it in one dose—without ever realizing what just happened.

It would be naïve to attribute Trump's rise to his showbiz skills. A simple proof of that is what was transpiring on the Democratic side. The events unfolding on the Democratic Party side begged the possibility of a different explanation. In the Democratic circles a similar story was unfolding. A senator who was barely known outside of Vermont was challenging the mighty Clinton brand name. Like Trump, data scientists gave Senator Bernie Sanders very little chance to succeed. Sanders was considered noise—till the time came when this noise became so overwhelming that people began calling it a revolution. It galvanized the progressive base. It won against the Clinton campaign in many states and even challenged the Democrat Party to redefine its fundamental processes of electing a nominee. The Clinton camp had no choice but to take notice of this phenomenon.

The political tide of 2016 was unorthodox, unexpected, and unconventional—but it begged the question: what happened? Paul Samuelson, one of the greatest American economists and Nobel Prize holder, wrote: "It is not too much to say that the widespread creation of dictatorships and the resulting World War II stemmed in no small measure from the world's failure to meet this basic economic problem [the Great Depression] adequately" (Samuelson and Mankiw, 2009). In other words, when economic discontent deepens, public behavior can lead to radical outcomes. These anomalies are not random events. They tend to be a consequence of our inability to comprehend and respond to what people want. But what we fail to understand, machines pick up in no time and act upon that information.

While Trump and Sanders emerged on the polar opposite sides of several social issues, when it came to certain economic phenomenon their messages seemed perfectly synchronized. Specifically, both candidates complained about the state of the economy, loss of jobs to foreign countries, concentration of wealth with the few, unfavorable tax structures for the middle class, and international treaties that took jobs away from Americans. It appeared that voters from both parties had rejected the ideological and social issues and found the economic concerns as the common denominator in both Trump and Sanders campaigns. Clearly, the common economic theme of both Trump and Sanders was resonating with the voters. Tired of being bounced around between the ideological positions of the two parties, it appeared that voters were sending a message that their will matters. Intelligent machines can, and did, fill the ideological vacuum.

What is surprising is the fact that after decades of job losses—a perfectly predictable outcome of a policy of an open and interconnected globalized economy enabled by massive automation—the issue of manufacturing job loss still looms and defines our political debate and elections.

Why did we wait decades to address this central issue? Why do we still grapple with the policy outcomes that we could have easily predicted? We are still trying to debate solutions to problems that we should have known before even the problems arose. Why didn't we see that coming? Why didn't we prepare for that? And most importantly, when we know that people are dissatisfied, should we use and exploit that sentiment to increase social conflict to win elections or should we approach such issues from an ethical perspective? Unfortunately, we observe the rise of extreme and nationalistic movements in many countries—all enabled by the misuse of intelligent machines to increase fear, hate, and mistrust in populations.

Clearly the twentieth-century leadership model—which is still followed, unfortunately—does not prepare leaders to act responsibly to protect the interests of a common person. The power unleashed by unintelligent technological revolutions (ones that created machines that lacked intelligence) produced massive turmoil and discontinuity. The aftereffects led to major wars, famines, economic recessions, and depressions. The potential of intelligent automation to disrupt is enormous.

The leadership needed for this era is different and requires significantly more ethical commitment than before. The oppression from the industrial era exploitation must not be repeated in the new era of intelligent automation. While the Trump presidency remained controversial and culminated in a disgraceful mob attack on the Capitol building, it serves as a stark reminder that machines can set the tone and outcomes of elections. Since it is hard to imagine that interference by foreign adversaries or opportunistic domestic players can be curtailed, the responsibility of using or benefiting from such technological innovation lies with the leaders. Knowing their disruptive power, leaders must reject the use of machines to exploit, manipulate, or increase conflict. Exploiting voters or increasing social conflict, or selling your products or services by exploiting or manipulating customers is a form of epistemic oppression which must not be allowed to persist.

> LEADERSHIP INSIGHT 1: AI leaders understand that billions of people are depending upon their business and political leadership. If they make bad decisions, future generations will suffer. The consequences can be devastating for the peace and security of our world.

## A NEVER-SEEN-BEFORE CHANGE TAKES SHAPE

As Donald Trump's presidential bid was solidifying, thousands of miles away in the Four Seasons hotel in Seoul, South Korea, another competition was transpiring. Perhaps just as unpredictable as the rise of Donald Trump and Bernie Sanders, two parties were competing in a different kind of a competition. The stakes were high and the competitive intensity was nerve-wracking.

Humans are a versatile species. They learn, they adapt, they think, they invent. They are the masters of this planet and they have controlled this planet and its resources for thousands of years. Nearly 2,500 years ago in China, some members of the master species invented a game known as Go. For thousands of years the game Go provided intellectual stimulation and entertainment for humans.

Go is an interesting game. A strategy-centric board game, at one time it was used to train warriors in China and Japan and was thought of as a martial art. The game is played on a 19 × 19-squares space. Players can have unlimited number of white and black pieces (known as stones). They strategically place these stones, and the goal is to capture each other's stones as prisoners and gain as much territory as possible. Not very different than Trump trying to win states and capturing delegates, the game Go requires significant strategy, skill, imagination, and creativity.

But the game being played in Seoul, South Korea, was special. Watched by over a hundred million people, it was not just any game. It was not even like the typical championships played by Go masters. In this particular match though, the master of this planet, the human species, was being challenged by a computer.

Team Humans was represented by Lee Sedol, a 33-year-old champion of Go. Team computers was represented by AlphaGo, an AI-based system developed by Google's company Deep. Madhumita Murgia (2016) reported this monumental game for the *Telegraph* and wrote the following about Lee:

His style is considered uniquely creative, flamboyant, even risky. He wages battle on the board aggressively. He is part of a rarefied club of eight Go players who have won more than 1,000 matches in their lifetime. "In the world of Go, he is his own thing," a professional player said to me, in wonder.

But today, on a crisp March afternoon, Lee has just lost one of the most important games of his life. The winner of the competition is a computer program called AlphaGo. This is the first time a machine has beaten a Go professional of the highest calibre.

"Today I am speechless," Lee told a room packed with reporters, photographers and Go professionals who had assembled in Seoul from around the world to witness his loss. "I really feel that AlphaGo played the near-perfect game."

An intelligent being, with the powers to rule the planet for thousands of years, just lost a game against another intelligent being—except the latter was not a human. The game was not a match of physical strength—the kind of battle that may have taken place in the times of Roman gladiators—it was a game of intellect. And intellect had been the sole attribute of humans, the one that distinguished them from animals, the one that gave them the power to conquer their world and beyond, the one that they had never found a parallel to. Murgia (2016) reports that Lee was in such a state of shock that he had to get up and leave the room. Perhaps it finally hit him that the humans now have a competitor. Perhaps he realized that humans finally have an equal, that possesses intelligence. The sole dominion of mankind has finally become a shared protectorate.

This game was consequential. Its meaning profoundly important, its implication far-reaching. What it does mean, however, is a simple fact that another species is now born, and it is intelligent. It will compete for capital, and it will compete against human capital. It will not have the same rights as humans do, its deployment will be domain-specific, its intelligence probably limited, and it may not have the vastness of the human intellect—but it does have sufficient intelligence to start changing things around. The point is that humans are no longer the only intelligent species living on this planet. We have a partner who will cohabit the planet with us.

As intelligent automation is brought into workplace, it is creating what can be classified as digital workers. These digital workers, like their human counterparts, participate in creating stakeholder value. Those who lead companies are now leading two types of workforce: digital and human. This implies that the existing leadership models, which were developed for twentieth-century-style bureaucratic organizations, are no longer applicable. A new leadership model is needed.

> LEADERSHIP INSIGHT 2: The adoption of AI technology will accelerate. It is impractical to assume that technological research, development, applications, and adoption will be halted in both civilian and military applications. Business and military interests will drive rapid adoption. Our world has entered a new phase of progress. A new type of leader is needed.

## NOT JUST ABOUT PROGRESS, PEOPLE MATTER

"I could stand in the middle of Fifth Avenue and shoot somebody, and I wouldn't lose any voters," an unapologetic Trump told the national media. Anger ripped through the traditional Republican circles as Trump made several politically offensive statements. Many politicians felt a strange right of entitlement over the Republican party and they saw Trump as trespassing on their conservative territory. Many had a hard time to come to terms with the fact that Donald Trump would run on the Republican ticket. The Republican establishment launched a fierce attack against Trump. Millions were spent to present Trump as too incompetent, too liberal, too crude, too un-presidential to be a president. Despite all that, the Trump phenomenon continued to find its inspiration among voters.

Donald Trump keeps no prisoners. When someone pulls a punch on him, he responds back. When someone attacks him, he attacks them right back. His style of blatant comments didn't cost him any states. He marched on as an astute warrior, winning the Republican nomination. When he debated, he debated furiously. When he spoke to audiences, he spoke without a teleport. It was as if he was talking from his heart, uncut and unedited. Political correctness, politician's astuteness, and political expediency were exchanged in favor of bluntness and even crudeness. Despite the crudeness, it was clear that people were truly paying attention to his rhetoric. The Republican establishment stood puzzled and horrified as it helplessly stared in shock on the sudden rise of Trump. But intelligent machines laid the groundwork for such a revolution. The American public was ready for a change.

Perhaps the reality is that both Trump and Bernie Sanders understood the anxiety of the American public. The amalgamation of three forces—information technology revolution, globalization, and the Great

Recession—had created tremendous mistrust. Americans no longer believed that their government was capable of protecting their interests. Traumatized by what transpired in the last three decades, Americans were not ready to allow the 2016 election to follow the old path. The status quo had to change. AI is good at identifying the dormant suffering of the masses and bringing such pains to surface.

After all, it was not that long ago when in America unintelligent machines churned, roiled, and swiveled voraciously, when conveyer belts spun dutifully as the rhythmic sounds of metal and gears captivated workers, and when the smell of grease and oil mixed with the odor of perspiration to define a strong middle class. That was the time when workers swarmed through brightly lit plants, creating intense activity, as powerful social interaction between workers established comradery and lasting bonds among them. These machines were the economic generators that powered America and allowed multiple generations of Americans to live with dignity and prosperity.

But in a matter of three decades, as if waking up from a blissful dream to a dreadful reality, forces of change sucked life out of America.

Manufacturing plants that were once packed with vibrancy of life and activity went silent and degenerated into rundown ruins. Neighborhoods turned into shabby ghost towns. As America was trying to get adjusted to this new reality and when the dust from previous storms had not even settled, a new economic hurricane developed and shattered the last glimpses of hope for many Americans. The Great Recession of 2008 ferociously landed and stabbed in the heart of American middle class. Like a final blow to bring the giant down, it delivered the knockout punch. Not just companies, this time around entire cities joined the ranks to file bankruptcies. Foreclosure signs popped up in the front yards of countless homes, as doors and windows were fettered with nailed wood panels to block entry, as money dried out for businesses, as labels on manufactured goods that once said Made in America were replaced by Made in China, and as services sector joined the manufacturing sector to shed jobs—a sense of deep hopelessness spread across America. The American dream seemed frail and fragile—almost lifeless. While their country was plunging and the American dream crushing cataclysmically, through the lens of intelligent social media, Americans watched in envy at the prosperity and growth of other countries. The high-risers of Beijing and Mumbai signified the transfer of power and wealth. As Americans struggled with their monthly car payments and faced repossessions, the images of young happy couples in developing economies buying expensive cars and photographing their triumphs on the front porches of luxury car dealers became a daily occurrence. The burgeoning middle class in other countries declared a clear victory over the dwindling middle class of America – and it was captured live on social media.

Perhaps Americans didn't want to be viewed as the collateral damage of policies defined by shifting priorities or ugly rivalries between the two parties. Perhaps they finally wanted a voice in issues that affect their well-being and lives.

In the past, though, it appears that business planning and policy making in the United Sates generally followed this line of logic: (a) we will set the business strategy or policy to take advantage of a certain social, economic, or political phenomenon (e.g., information technology, globalization); (b) it will benefit many Americans; (c) it will hurt many Americans; (d) in the end those who are hurt will adapt, somehow; (e) as they adapt, eventually the self-correcting mechanism will make everything okay; (f) up until the time they adapt and the self-correcting mechanism manifests, we will ignore their plight.

This line of thinking appears to be common in our policy planning and business strategy development. While we have dedicated resources to conduct war games to preemptively study wars, why do we fail to apply the same concept in major policy or business strategy decisions. Why don't we simulate the aftereffects of our policy decisions? And if we do understand those consequences then why don't we put in place support structures around policies to minimize the collateral damage?

One of the major concerns raised in this book is that the fourth industrial revolution—the introduction of AI—is a more powerful and profound change than any change that has ever taken place in the human history—and that we cannot afford to enter the fourth revolution with the self-defeating mindset.

We cannot quell progress in the name of responsibility and nor can we achieve it by being irresponsible. Both need to go hand in hand and this book shows how to keep that balance.

The consequences for human civilization are too grave. If we approach the AI revolution as we have approached other changes in our recent history, we will create unparalleled destruction. Unlike the economic hiccups or cycles, this change will not only redefine the economic and social fabric of the human civilization but also unleash the most powerful force we have ever encountered on our planet. To approach and manage this change, we need to be extremely vigilant and cautious.

A new type of leader is needed to lead in this uncertain world. Above all, this leader needs to be extremely cognizant of his or her responsibility to the people of this world.

LEADERSHIP INSIGHT 3: In our zeal to score big, we sometimes forget or ignore the interests of the common person. When making technology decisions, "people" (the human factor) must be included as part of the equation. AI leaders would always remember that AI exists for the benefit of people.

## AI NEEDS NEW TYPES OF LEADERS

Today, we stand on the eve of a new revolution unfolding. This revolution is not only different than anything that we have ever experienced before, but it is also highly powerful. Inventing intelligence is a powerful thing. The issue is that as a society—as individuals, as businesses, as industries, as non-profits, as governments—we are not ready for this change.

*Washington Post*'s journalist Luke Sharrett noticed that the so-called strong and too-good-to-be-true US economy has not reached all Americans—a fact acknowledged by Jerome H. Powell, chair of the Federal Reserve. There are deep structural problems in the US economy that remained uncured, Sharett argued. Sharett provided many statistics. For example, 40 percent of American adults say they don't have savings of $400 to cover emergency expenses. The labor force participation for men aged 25–54 remains lower than pre-Great-Recession period. Average pay has declined in many sectors. The suicide rates are up, and life expectancy is declining.

In the midst of today's volatile modern economy, an economy whose most consistent feature has been a major recession every few years, we are dropping a powerful new shockwave of cognitive automation. Cognitive automation is capable of automating all human work—physical or mental. While daily tweets, sarcasm, cyber bullying, and taunts have become a new normal in American policy making and politics, the common person has never faced a more dire future. The tools that once professed to empower the common man or woman have now turned into the tool of manipulation and exploitation. The voice of the common person has been submerged and crushed under the overwhelming burden of content, data, and algorithms. In this environment, understanding of the threats and problems created by AI is greatly lacking.

LEADERSHIP INSIGHT 4: Irresponsible adoption and development impacts everyone. By being responsible, businesses can accomplish both: maximize business results and minimize social costs. The optimal strategy for leaders is responsible automation.

## WHAT BECOMES OF LEADERSHIP?

In 2008 and 2012, Senator, and later president, Obama's campaign teams had used the power of the big data to identify and drive the voters to the ballot boxes. Being able to study the voters and voter behavior, carve out niches and target potential voters were innovations made possible using the data. In some ways, it was the application of marketing knowhow to win elections. But 2016 was nothing like that.

In the 2016 elections, based upon the testimony of a former FBI agent Clint Watts before the Senate Intelligence Committee, Russia used armies of Twitter bots to spread fake news. Clearly, in a matter of few years, the technology of how to win elections had moved forward from big data to big data plus AI. Some of these bots posed themselves as Republican swing voters from Midwest and attempted to "social engineer" voters—the testimony stated.

If true, such a use of technology goes beyond the innocuous use of data to dissect and segment markets or voters. It is something that humankind has never encountered before. This implies that semi-rational and intelligent agents, to a large degree autonomous, that are designed to learn and adapt can offer powerful tools for leaders. These tools can influence and persuade as no human can.

Just as the power of this technology shattered the old model of how to win elections, it throws a monkey wrench in the existing management and leadership theories. In fact, in some ways it dismantles all the previous work in the leadership studies. The charisma, the situational awareness, the situational intervention, the servant, the follower-leader connection, the transformational leadership—all require some type of reevaluation.

Before we jump into the requirements of leadership in the AI era, we would like to raise some provocative questions to demonstrate how leaders can exploit the cognitive era.

- If a technology can learn, adapt, formulate goals, and independently influence people with goals that it has formulated on its own, does that change the role and structure of leadership?
- What if a technology can completely conceal its identity, and can shape and present the "image" of a leader that is far from reality, and via social engineering convince masses to follow the leader, does that require a reassessment of leadership?
- If such technologies can only be accessed by those with significant resources, is it possible that the voice and face of true and ethical leader may never be

heard? Would leadership then really come down to owning and managing powerful bots—both for influence and producing results?

This means that leaders must not only develop superior business strategies and have strong ethical commitment, but they must also develop a deeper self-awareness. Ethics, from that perspective, are not just about following a model printed in a book. They become inwardly focused. They are derived from the deep internal understanding and personal psyche.

Clearly, a new model of leadership is needed to showcase the leader for the AI era. As mentioned by Jeff Adams in the interview at the start of the chapter, *"Automation should lift employees' spirits and morale."*

CHAPTER 2

# INTELLIGENCE COMES ALIVE

*The measure of intelligence is in the ability to change.*

—ALBERT EINSTEIN

**EXECUTIVE INTERVIEW 2**

**Gaurav Khanna, CEO of Sky Cybernetics**

Authors: How would you describe the current state of artificial intelligence (AI) in your industry?

*Khanna: Agriculture is both a foundation and a major industry of the economy in most of the countries. AI technology is rapidly rectifying the problems while recommending specific action that is required to overcome the problem. To find the solutions quickly AI is efficient in monitoring the information. AI is being used in agriculture to improve results with a minimal environmental cost. By implementing AI, farmers can monitor soils and identify a disease with 98 percent accuracy. Thus, AI helps farmers to monitor the fruit and vegetable by adjusting the light to accelerate production.*

- **Forecast Weather Data**

*The forecast data help farmers increase yields and profits without risking the crop. The analysis of the data generated helps the farmer to take the precaution by understanding and learning with AI. By implementing such practice helps to make a smart decision on time.*

- **Monitoring Crop and Soil Health**

*AI is the best tool to monitor the health of soil. Adoption of AI is an efficient way to identify possible flaws and nutrient deficiencies in the soil. With the image recognition approach* while using various algorithms, AI identifies possible defects through images captured by the camera. With the help of AI machine learning and deep learning, applications are developed to analyze flora patterns in agriculture. Such AI-enabled applications are supportive in understanding soil conditions, diseases, and plant pests.

- **Decrease Pesticide Usage**

Farmers can use AI to manage weeds by implementing computer vision, mobile App, drone, robotics, and machine learning. By implementing AI, data are gathered to keep a check on the weed which helps the farmers to spray pesticides and other chemicals only where the weeds are present to certain part of field and not entire field. This directly reduced the usage of the chemical spraying to whole field. As a result, AI reduces herbicide usage in the field compared to the volume of chemicals normally sprayed.

- **AI Agriculture Tools such as Apps, Bots, and Drones**

AI-enabled agriculture App and bots help farmers to find more efficient ways to protect their crops from weeds. This is also helping to overcome the labor challenge. AI bots in the agriculture field can harvest crops at a higher volume and faster pace than human laborers. By leveraging computer vision helps to monitor the weed and spray them. Thus, AI is helping farmers find more efficient ways to protect their crops from weeds.

Hence AI is helping the farmers to monitor their crops without the need to be physically present in the farm. Now many enterprises and start-ups are looking forward to AI development in agriculture. AI is redefining the traditional pattern of agriculture. The future of AI in agriculture is way ahead in offering radical transformation with advanced approaches.

Authors: In what way has AI transformed your organization?

*Khanna:* Our old job descriptions—engineer, product manager, designer—are breaking down. For example, if you look at any mobile app, there was probably a product manager that drew a simplified diagram called a wireframe to design that app. But if you look at detecting disease through drone or monitoring soil condition in farms, you don't need a wireframe for a self-driving car. That just doesn't make as much sense. So we're inventing and working on development of brand-new processes and workflows for the AI era as well. I think that true AI organizations are much more sophisticated, much more strategic in data acquisition. So, for example, I've done things like launch a product in one geography to acquire data then take to the next geography. But then we don't monetize any of this.

*If you can just have enough data to launch a product that's good enough, that allows you to enter a positive feedback loop in which your users help you generate more data. More data makes the product even better, so you have more users. And that positive feedback loop allows you to accumulate data, so that maybe after a few years you could have a pretty defensible business.*

Authors: How is AI creating value for your firm?

*Khanna: As we all know, the volume of data that we have created as human beings have grown exponentially in the last few years. We start having more and more devices that can create, send, store, and save data—we can just look at our mobile phones, and how powerful they have become in the last few years.*
*With that in mind, it is not a necessity, or a must, to have AI analytics implemented across the whole company, but rather there where it makes the most sense: where we have large amounts of data, or where it simply is going to have the best ROI (ROI = Return of Investment). After all, when looked through the eyes of the business—if it doesn't add any value, or provides something in return—there is no need for certain implementation, most probably.*

Authors: What do you think are current organizational challenges relating to AI?

*Khanna: As has been seen, most of the companies have mainly been experimenting with the possibilities, introducing "AI" into certain operations and business use cases but on a limited scale.*
*The most mature achievements have happened mostly in risk management and compliance and secondly in customer engagement, very rarely in all other domains. About these mature AI systems, only 30 percent of these firms have confirmed however that they have been "fully deployed" at scale in their organization. All other use cases are still in a stage between initial experiments and small-scale deployments.*
*Even within a single field, conditions are always changing from one section to the next. Unpredictable weather, soil quality, pests and disease affect farming worldwide. Growers may feel their prospects are good for an upcoming harvest, but until that day arrives, the outcome will always be uncertain.*

### A. Data Is Biased

*Bias is one of the biggest challenges facing AI. While everyone strives for accurate data and absolute facts, AI biases do exist. Bad data is often laced with racial, gender, communal, or ethnic biases.*

### B. Collecting Only Relevant Data

*For an organization to successfully implement AI strategies and programs, they must have a base set of data and maintain a constant source of relevant data to ensure that AI can be useful in their selected industry. Data can be collected on various applications with a multitude of formats such as text, audio, images, and videos. The wide range of platforms to collect this data adds to the challenges of artificial intelligence. In order to be successful, all these data must be integrated in a manner that the AI can understand and transform into useful results.*

### C. Manpower

*The challenge is sourcing the skills necessary for artificial intelligence development: "With talent being one of the biggest challenges to AI, no matter how advanced a company's digital program, it's perhaps not surprising that companies are leaving no stone unturned when sourcing people and skills."*

Authors: What is not being done right in the AI revolution?

Khanna:

- *Recent AI advances, while seemingly impressive, are very narrow in scope and require a lot of human supervision and input to work in real applications.*
- *While as many as 45 percent of current jobs contain tasks that may be automatable, less than 8 percent of jobs will be fully automatable by 2030.*
- *The actual percentage of jobs that will be automated will be lower, because technology adoption lags behind technology development due to costs in implementation, maintenance, and overcoming cultural and regulatory hurdles.*
- *Like with many new technologies that came before, many AI tools will augment and not replace workers by automating subtasks of a job. This augmentation may raise demand in some industries while depressing wages in others.*
- *For the jobs that AI will displace, the impact will vary greatly across countries, industries, education levels, socioeconomic status, age, and gender. These disparities may have socially and politically destabilizing effects.*
- *To alleviate short-term economic impact, it is important for governments to enact policies that value human capital and help displaced workers transition to new jobs in growing industries, such as healthcare and education.*

Authors: Where do you think opportunities exist with regard to AI in the workplace?

*Khanna:* Much time is spent in conference calls and meetings, leaving precious little time for creative work. In the future, AI algorithms could communicate with each other to determine the best time of day to schedule calls and meetings.

Office space is expensive and many companies promote working remotely (either at home, when traveling, or at customer locations). Sharing desks and office space can be extremely efficient but requires complex scheduling. AI systems could learn work patterns to optimally allocate desk space on demand, making better use of physical space while keeping workers inspired, engaged, and productive.

Technical support personnel are very expensive and often deal with customers who are unhappy or in moments of crisis. Recognizing the sensitivity of these situations, AppleCare encourages its staff to be warm and friendly on the phone. While the front-end staff reassure customers, back-end technicians do the diagnosis.

Making decisions is the primary job of a CEO, for whom it is vital to avoid bias and remain objective. In the future, an AI-based system could support this working as an "AI-based devil's advocate" that challenges decisions with insightful questions, exposing the CEO with alternative viewpoints, throwing "high-quality curveballs" to enable more creative and critical thinking.

Authors: In your opinion, what should and what should not be automated? Why?

*Khanna:*

### A. Automation in Farming

*Traditional methods used by farmers aren't sufficient enough to serve the increasing demand and so they have to hamper the soil by using harmful pesticides in an intensified manner. Automation of farming practices has proved to increase the gain from the soil and also has strengthened the soil fertility.*

### B. Automation in Health Industry

*It puts consumers in control of health and well-being. Additionally, AI increases the ability for healthcare professionals to better understand the day-to-day patterns and needs of the people they care for, and with that understanding they are able to provide better feedback, guidance, and support for staying healthy.*

## C. Identity Management

*Cities can become safer when images are effectively captured, assessed and matched. Facial recognition tools can recognize anyone with an arrest warrant out on the loose. Tracking and correlating individual journeys. Monitoring real-time data against specific parameters. Self-controlling decision-making shouldn't be automated*
*Once the self-controlling decision-making starts happening within the machine it will be difficult to control the machine. Machine may give harmful instruction to robotics and could lead to severe damage to society.*

Authors: How should companies prioritize AI projects? How are you doing it?

*Khanna: Before you tell your AI engineers to start coding (or contract an AI company to do so), there is one last thing you need to verify. You need to validate the assumptions you have made—both from a business as well as from a technical perspective. Among others, you should answer the following questions:*

- *Which factors are driving the value of the use case?*
- *How much data is needed? Do you really have the data and is it accessible?*
- *Which level of accuracy is needed and is it achievable?*

*Furthermore, you should do an ethical and legal due diligence of the use cases: Make sure that the use case is not doing harm and is in compliance with the laws of your country. At this stage of the process, you need to balance a further detailing of the use case with speed. When developing a rough business case for an AI application, insisting on a detailed business plan is not always helpful. But when you are just about to start the execution phase, there should be no more doubts or open questions.*

Authors: What are some of the best practices you've seen with regard to AI in the workplace?

*Khanna:*
*Do: emphasize the narrowness of today's AI-powered programs*
*Do: avoid comparisons to pop culture depictions of AI*
*Systems are complex and their actions are difficult to interpret. There is research done in that field, but there is still a long way to go. But as with any other technology we use it as soon as it kind of works, even if there are well-known risks (like nuclear power) and uncertainties. The term AI attributes unexpected system behavior (i.e., a Tesla car suddenly stops with no apparent reason) to a "conscious decision" of "The AI" instead of a not-yet understood behavior of a complex technical system.*

Authors: Companies are part of an economic ecosystem including various stakeholders such as other companies, government, academia, and others. What role do stakeholders need to play to help AI flourish in companies?

Khanna:

1. *Investors—owners, bank, or investment company*
2. *Business people—in companies working cross-culturally in your business or industry*
3. *Business consultant—someone with specialist knowledge*
4. *Colleagues—management and staff*
5. *Customers—those likely to be your clients*
6. *Suppliers—of essential materials and services for your business*
7. *Community—local society and also the physical environment*
8. *Cultural expert—someone with insight into engaging with local community*
9. *Government official—someone who can give you insight and be an advocate for you*
10. *Body of Christ—local church community, mission organizations and supporting churches*
11. *Spiritual advisor or mentor—someone with wise counsel you can be accountable to*
12. *God—the most important stakeholder*


Authors: What do you think are essential leadership attributes in the AI revolution? Why?

Khanna:

### Agility

*Due to the speed of change in the future workplace, leaders will have to be agile and able to embrace and celebrate change. Successful leaders during the fourth industrial revolution will see change not as a burden but as an opportunity to grow and innovate.*

### Emotional Intelligence (EQ)

*Just as employees will need a healthy amount of emotional intelligence, it will be critical for leaders in the future workplace to be able to perceive, understand, and manage emotions—theirs and their team's.*

> **Humble Confidence**
>
> *Tomorrow's leaders will need to find a balance between confidence in their own abilities and decisions, and being humble about their place in the organization. Future leaders will take all the unique skills of the team working together to drive initiatives and leaders won't be viewed as the critical cog to success. Tomorrow's leaders will encourage others to shine.*
>
> **Quick Learners**
>
> *Leaders will need to quickly assess a situation and learn what they need in order to make effective decisions. Along with this, they will need to be open to coaching and learning from the subject matter experts on their team.*
>
> Authors: What do you think is the future of AI in the workplace? How will work be transformed?
>
> *Khanna: AI agent may automatically respond to simple e-mail requests and another may manage your appointments.*
> *AI will allow the constant monitoring—perhaps bordering on surveillance—of the workplace and the employees in the workplace. This has many potential downsides with regard to employee freedoms and privacy, but has lots of benefits both for the employer and employee. It will lead to a more effective and productive work environment.*
> *The digital spreadsheet will revolutionize the planning of budgets, working forward with initial estimates and then backward to adjust expenses to match available resources.*

Despite the rise of television programming services, certain older television shows continue to attract millions of viewers. One of these shows is Jeopardy. In Jeopardy, people compete to win prizes worth tens of thousands of dollars. The game allows participants to select categories. Once players select a category, the game provides answers to questions and the competitors have to guess the questions for which the answers are provided. An extremely popular show, Jeopardy attracts nearly nine million viewers daily.

In February of 2011, IBM decided to compete in one of the Jeopardy shows. After all, IBM—the big blue, one of the icons of American leadership in technology—was going to send its best and the brightest. Jeopardy organizers, on the other hand, searched for their best ever champions and identified two men who were to take on the IBM nominee. The fascinating part of the game was that instead of sending a human, IBM was represented by a computer named Watson. But Watson is not just any computer. It is a smart computer that can learn and reason.

In front of the classic blue background of Jeopardy, three contestants stood behind their podiums. Watson was in the middle and was represented by a screen showing a globe with five lines on the top and as Watson thought, the screen moved to indicate that Watson was thinking. And the fact of the matter is that Watson was indeed thinking.

For three days, the intense competition continued. The ferociousness of opponents, the competitive spirit, and the clash of players amid cheers and claps thrilled the audiences across the world. The game moved back and forth as triumph alternated between humans and the computer, but the computer slowly, but surely, laid the claim to the trophy. It was as if each day it was getting smarter and better. On the third day, the computer decisively snatched the victory in its favor and left the humans defeated and disgraced. The master race was beaten by its own creation. Watson didn't clinch its victory from the jaws of defeat, instead it showed that humans stood no chance against the computer.

The end result of the competition was not too different than what Lee experienced in Seoul. Watson won and humans lost. First time in the history of human civilization the trophy of intelligence was stolen from humans and handed over to another being. A new winner had been crowned and it was not a human.

When thought in those terms, it is an extraordinary challenge for humankind and for which we are not ready. The change is happening faster than our ability to comprehend. From financial markets to political institutions, AI will restructure the very functional dynamics of our world. A new type of leader is needed to take charge.

## THE ERA OF INTELLIGENT AUTOMATION

One way to think about what is transpiring in modern business is to view the current transformation in terms of the industrial revolutions. The first two industrial revolutions were driven by the power of steam engine and then electromechanical power.

It is important to realize—specially for younger people who have experienced and continue to experience the power of the Internet—that the auto sector was no less of a revolution than the Internet. It is because of automobiles that we have malls and retail, manufacturing and distribution, hospitals, and even services sector in which people commute to work. The ability to efficiently move people, goods, and raw materials transformed our world and economy.

Then began the information revolution, which led to the creation of the Internet. In the three revolutions, the common denominator was that machines were always subservient to human command. Incapable of learning or accumulating experience, machines did not have a mind of their own. They functioned under the strict commands of humans and only when they broke down, they stopped obeying the commands. But unlike their ancestors from the first three revolutions, machines now have the ability to be autonomous.

The cognitive revolution, the one we are in now, has altered the definition of what a machine is. Machine is no longer just an automation device, it is now a thinking companion. This era of cognitive machines is known as the cognitive revolution (aka fourth industrial revolution or AI revolution or intelligent automation revolution). Some scientists believe that by 2030 or so, we will be able to create machines that will have self-consciousness and that will launch the consciousness revolution. Others think that a lot more time will be needed to have human-type machines.

## AI in Terms of Industrial Revolutions

| Industrial Revolution I | Industrial Revolution II | Information Revolution | Cognitive Revolution | Consciousness Revolution |
|---|---|---|---|---|
| Textile manufacturing and steam engine | Division of labor and mass production, with electrical energy. Mass Distribution. Steel production, automobiles, and electricity | IT and electronics that automate production, solve problems, and connect (Internet) | Functional/Task specific or Narrow AI Machines that automate cognitive processes and physical work (human and superhuman level) | Strong or General AI |
| 1760 | 1850 | 1950 | 2011 | 2030 |

Rough Timeframe – Not Scaled

Cognitive revolution is marked by the functional or narrow AI which means that solutions are developed with narrow or specific applications vs. strong or general AI, which means machines become intelligent like humans and develop self-awareness. Narrow AI does not mean that machines are not smarter than humans in certain tasks. In fact, they can be far more intelligent and efficient than humans in narrow applications or tasks; it is just that they just don't have the diversity, flexibility, and range of intelligence displayed by humans.

## THE WINTERS OF INTELLIGENT AUTOMATION

America was enjoying a well-deserved economic boom. A decade had passed since Japan and Germany surrendered and World War II came to an end; the Korean War had ended; and the nuclear era had begun. The anti-communist sentiment was raging strong. Swinging the pendulum of conservatism to extreme, McCarthyism was setting new and ugly standards for political repression and fear mongering. One of the most unlikely victims of reactionary forces of social change was the comic books industry. Viewed as a promoter of immorality, the comic industry was attacked from different angles. Despite the stigmatizing attacks, the industry survived and even prospered—and most importantly it gave us a new and powerful fascination with superheroes and intelligent machines. A little more than half a century later, that fascination has become the largest contributor of storylines in the movie industry and that turned it into multibillion movie franchises (for example *Iron Man*).

Just around the time when America was in love-hate relationship with superheroes, a bunch of professors and researchers decided to hold a conference on an interesting upcoming technology—intelligence in computers. In the summer of 1956, this conference turned into a month-long event at Dartmouth, and that is where the term "artificial intelligence" was coined.

What is so profound about this conference is not that the participants came up with the name *artificial intelligence* but because they had not experienced the modern computers (as we know them today), they had not seen Google or Microsoft or Intel or Cisco. But they had the powerful imagination to conceptualize a future for intelligent machines.

They set some aggressive goals for AI and while their imagination was powerful, their ability to predict when the reality will unfold was not. The AI industry went through periods of ups and downs and bounced between waves of optimism followed by dips of disappointments. When disappointments happened, investment dried out and support for the field dwindled. These periods of investment stagnation in the field are known as the winters of AI. But as happened in Narnia, forces were lining up to end the winters forever.

But to claim that prior to the current rise of cognitive technologies, AI failed commercially altogether is inaccurate. After all, even Google's search algorithm is an intelligent algorithm. Despite the investment backlash experienced during the "winters of AI" the AI community continued to work toward creating new products and services. The community became more integrated and unlike other fields in which researchers had to wait months and even years before they could publish an article, the AI community developed protocols to rapidly publish and share research directly or present and publish papers in conferences and make them available for everyone. This fast sharing of information propelled the research and development efforts. In this open and shared learning environment, powerful and transformative innovation shaped the future of the field.

## THE FOUR FORCES THAT HELPED END THE AI WINTERS

Have you noticed that Hollywood seems to be fascinated with the power of an integrated four? Like *Ghostbusters* there seems to be many movies that show the power of four? *Fantastic Four*, *Teenage Mutant Ninja Turtles*, and the four hobbits in the *Lord of the Rings*. It is as if when the power of four gets united, it unleashes a powerful integrative force. Interestingly, there are four forces shaping the AI revolution:

**Connectivity and Network Capabilities:** Thanks to the advent of the Internet, today we live in a connected world. Created by a nexus of interdependent and complementary technologies—such as social media platforms, cloud, mobile technologies, web, and various other advanced software and hardware—this infrastructure has enabled us to connect as a civilization. Even though this connectivity is built upon a decentralized structure of various disparate, distributed, and functionally separate systems, it functions as a collective structure that augments and connects human consciousness at a global level. The other fascination aspect of this amazing structure is that it brings people and machines (e.g., Internet of Things (IoT)) together—that is, making machines a participant and a major stakeholder in this enormous conglomerate of connectivity. In this world, machines do more than simply being the calculators and processors of information—as they provide an augmented layer of consciousness as evaluators, decision-makers, partners, and even thoughtful creators of data and information.

**Processing and Analytical Capabilities:** Today, we also have tremendously powerful processing and analytical power in our computers. In a world that aimed to "connect" processing and analytical power increased the efficiency of the interactions, improved the quality of relationships, and enhanced the analytical rigor to gain deep insights about humans. It allowed us to move beyond storing analyzing structured data and enabled us to analyze the unstructured data (including image, sound, videos, etc.).

**Data and Data Management:** Specifically, two things happened with data. First, as a civilization we began recording and storing more data than we ever did. Second, we developed techniques to manage the data. Data management includes processes such as data governance, data quality management, metadata management, and master data management. These knowledge areas represent the logical structures of information and allow us to process and manipulate data faster and more efficiently.

**Algorithms:** A large part of AI is made possible by the algorithms. These algorithms help machines learn and constitute as the key elements of machine learning. Math departments from all over the world contributed, and continue to contribute, to develop algorithms that made new and more advanced applications of AI possible.

These four forces created a perfect environment for the arrival of a permanent spring in AI. It allowed the development of a wide variety of real applications and practical solutions. And it was not a coincidence that hundreds of billions of dollars of investment is now flowing into this field.

## THE WHOLE AI REVOLUTION AND WORK

How would AI alter the nature of work? This question can be addressed by first understanding what work is. Mankind had set itself apart from all those living things that shared the responsibility of pushing life forward. Perfecting the art of survival by learning how to maneuver through the never-ending ferocity and ruthless force of nature, life relied upon the evolutionary techniques such as natural selection and random mutations. In some ways, nature imposed survival challenges and also granted species a way to overcome those challenges via long and patient learning acquired through normal biological evolution.

The goalless evolution set the path and destiny in motion for millions of species and while all followed diligently, humans attempted to pursue a different path. Humans successfully and sustainably outmaneuvered nature by learning how to eliminate the persistent dependency of survival on the randomness of evolution and instead opted to tame the nature and fight back. Daring to take control, blocking and tackling, and eliminating the ties that once made the survival of this species utterly dependent upon evolutionary forces, humans set themselves apart from other species.

Lifting the bondage of evolution and ending their colossal dependency on evolution to master survival, humans had set themselves free to master the survival skills on their own. They could now accelerate adaptation, albeit synthetic, but nonetheless effective. They could now tame the nature and block the monstrosity that it inflicted upon them. But such a synthetic adaptation came with a cost. "Work" became the cost of survival as humans needed to work to survive and overcome nature.

Work on its own ontological front required the necessary amalgamation of both cognitive and physical abilities as neither was sufficient on its own to overcome the obstacles of nature or to craft synthetic adaptation. For example, while writing computer code is a cognitive ability, a computer programmer needs to type, which is a physical activity. Similarly, digging a hole may require significant physical work but also requires cognitive abilities to determine where, how deep, and how best to dig a hole. Thus, work can be viewed as a point on a two-dimensional space because of physical and cognitive abilities.

Work also required a certain level of cooperation and social structure to materialize. What work produced were the artifacts of human creativity—tools and machines—that simplified work further and that made humans gain superior control and an edge over nature. Thus, at the center of mankind's core battle of survival in its ongoing war against nature, work and machines acquired the central place.

To document and analyze its adventures and encounters with cognitive and physical work and survival, with machines and the various consequences of machines and the social dynamics of work, mankind developed social sciences. Thus, social sciences—such as sociology, economics, political science, organizational research, and psychology—became the medium through which humankind debated on what constitutes as a superior method to facilitate survival, and to engineer synthetic and accelerated adaptation, of delivering surplus, and of designing a society to constitute the sustainability of ambitious endeavors to conquer nature. However, the silent underlying assumptions of social sciences that

a. work is necessary to create survival value;
b. machines simplify physical and cognitive work but lack the ability to conceptualize and create either cognitive or physical work; and
c. modern social, economic, and political processes and structures are all built around the concept of machine

remained unchanged throughout the spectrum of social sciences.

The unshakable implicitness was so basic that they required no explicit mention in literature. Such were the simplicity and matter-of-factness of these assumptions that no one really cared to list them as the underlying assumptions.

They were not conjectures or speculative as their validity and explicitness was derived from their obviousness. They were just there—like gravity—which is there but typically doesn't require specific mention in social sciences research.

The most consequential issue of our times is that these underlying assumptions are now being challenged. The emerging reality of our time is that

a. traditional work may no longer be necessary to create survival value as the work going forward will now be to eliminate work completely;
b. machines may be able to not only perform advanced cognitive and physical functions but also conceptualize and create work; and
c. the definition of machine may get altered.

This foundational change implies that the fundamentals of social sciences would be altered and that the consequences of such a change are enormous. The advent and rise of AI will challenge, deconstruct, and even shatter the underlying assumptions.

The above changes have a significant impact on management and leadership.

The integration of AI and robotics in the workplace has merits and demerits for the organization. For most, the appeal lies in productivity enhancement through improved data gathering and processing as well as customer service improvements. It contributes to operational efficiencies. The danger lies in the ensuing organizational changes that take place—workforce displacement, poor planning and integration, and inefficient management systems, among others.

This implies that having innovative technologies such as AI and robotics in the workplace is just half the story—the other half is about getting it to work well in order to reap its full benefits.

## AI LEADERS SHOULD INVEST IN THE FOUR FORCES

AI leaders need to understand that investing in digital transformation and information technology are not enough. Intelligent automation, enabled by the four forces described in the previous section, is the new source of competitive advantage for companies.

These four forces—processing power, algorithms, data, and safe and intelligent connectivity—requires its own plan and investment. Such plans are more than the standard IT plans. They are known as intelligent automation plans and they are driven by adopting AI technologies such as machine learning.

Hold a meeting and get a review of the following:

- **Data:** If you have a data management organization, ask the organization to develop and provide the following analysis: Can your enterprise easily access and use the data needed? How are the governance standards of data? What is the data quality? What types of unstructured, structured, and dark data exist in your organization? What is your null data? What investment will be needed to accomplish your set goals?
- **Processing Power:** Ask your IT department to give you an overview of the organizational processing power. Are you using latest GPUs? Are you using cloud? What infrastructure exists?
- **Connectivity:** What connectivity challenges exist in your firm? Are cyber security measures in place? How can performance be optimized? What are anticipated future needs?
- **Algorithms**: Do you have proper manpower and related resources in place to create the best algorithms? What changes need to take place? What development plans are necessary?

Gaurav Khanna mentioned in the chapter interview that "it is not a necessity, or a must, to have AI analytics implemented across the whole company, but rather where it makes the most sense." With the AI revolution, organizations have the opportunity to enhance their cognitive strengths and make intelligence come to life. However, this does not happen by mere chance; careful thought and planning along with forward thinking leadership is necessary.

CHAPTER 3

# A LEADER WHO TAMES MACHINES

*The first ultra-intelligent machine is the last invention that man need ever make, provided that the machine is docile enough to tell us how to keep it under control.*

—NICK BOSTROM

---

**EXECUTIVE INTERVIEW 3**

**Raphael Danilo, Cofounder and CEO, Yobs**

Authors: How would you describe the current state of artificial intelligence (AI) in your industry?

*Danilo: AI in HR is still in its infancy. The last five years saw the first global rollouts of automation for low-complexity tasks like interview scheduling, resume screening and basic conversational chatbots. For the next five years, the industry will be defined by rollouts of AI technology to support more complex HR tasks. These include tasks like talent assessments, both behavioral and technical. It also includes various types of recommendation engines to support mobility, promotions and learning and development initiatives.*

Authors: In what way has AI transformed your organization?

*Danilo: A combination of AI and domain expertise is at the core of our organization at Yobs. The Yobs talent assessment API enables organizations to tap into a network of trained Industrial/Organizational (I/O) Psychologists to conduct behavioral assessments remotely. In turn, these I/O professionals are supported by our Natural Language Processing technology which helps standardize and de-bias the assessment results provided by these professionals.*

*Our clients leverage the assessment API to identify high-performers beyond the resume, and support talent management decisions with validated science that is expensive, difficult and time-consuming to traditionally access.*

Authors: How is AI creating value for your firm?

*Danilo: We utilize AI in a couple of key areas at Yobs. First, we use Natural Language Processing to standardize and augment the work of real I/O professionals in conducting talent assessments. Our machine learning (ML) models then learn from every assessment and interaction between these trained professionals and the end-user in order to reduce costs and streamline talent assessment processes by up to 80 percent, saving organizations millions of dollars in lost productivity and poor decisions.*

Authors: What do you think are current organizational challenges relating to AI?

*Danilo: The three core challenges related to AI in HR are usability, privacy, and explainability.*

*Firstly, many AI-powered vendors require organizations to essentially hand over all their data in hopes of getting value from the tool, which creates major risks and is simply not feasible.*

*Secondly, unless proper steps are taken to protect and account for the personal and demographic data of users, organizations and vendors risk to create biased models and put personal information in jeopardy. At Yobs, we anonymize user data and constantly perform validation studies to ensure our assessments are free of systemic bias.*

*Finally, it is critical for AI products to not be a "black box" to the customer and end user. The way predictions are obtained and on which dataset they are trained should not be opaque to the end user. It is both possible and desirable for vendors to utilize techniques like supervised and reinforcement learning to build explainable and accurate prediction models. At Yobs for example, the prediction models learn from real experts, where the right and wrong answer is clearly defined for every interaction. This allows us to build explainable models at scale without the methodology and outputs being opaque to the end user.*

Authors: What is not being done right in the AI revolution?

*Danilo: In my opinion, overzealous AI vendors and sensationalist journalists covering AI are both doing a disservice to the industry they serve. The former focus purely on bottom-line profits, oftentimes disregarding the PR and legal risk they are putting their customers at. Meanwhile, the latter love to write sensational pieces on AI because it attracts readers, oftentimes on deeply technical and nuanced topics, but without spending the time to understand said nuances. This is doing a major disservice to organizations that could genuinely benefit from thoughtfully implementing technologies in their business processes.*

Authors: Where do you think opportunities exist with regard to AI in the workplace?

*Danilo: I believe the biggest issue facing our labor market is the one billion workers who need to be upskilled and reskilled over the next decade, due to occupations being transformed, and sometimes becoming obsolete. There is a massive opportunity to help these workers find meaningful work based on their innate behavioral strengths and potential within their organization or in a new career. A combination of thoughtful, science-based AI and real human expertise can be the solution to help organizations face this challenge.*

Authors: In your opinion, what should and what should not be automated? Why?

*Danilo: A rule of thumb I use is to first evaluate if there is "perfect information," and second whether success in the task at hand can be defined in rules. I use the game of chess as an example.*
*At any given time, the chess board offers perfect information because all the moves that have been made by each player and all the possible outcomes are known. Even if they are hard to conceptualize for the human brain, they are finite. So there is what we call "perfect information." This is why computers have been able to consistently beat even the top Chess player in the world given enough training data. The computer can essentially learn from millions of chess games and knows the rules by heart, which offers a clear advantage in this type of task.*
*In the workplace, we sometimes operate with near-perfect information. But more often than not, we are working with imperfect information. The more complex and hard to define the task is, the longer it will take for a computer to outperform a human who benefits from critical thinking. When we make hiring or promotion decisions for example, whether we realize it or not, we are making a prediction. We are predicting whether a candidate will make for a great customer success representative or engineer or manager using information like their work history, skills, references, and behavioral attributes. As we know, people will always underperform computer predictions in a perfect information game. However, in the workplace, it takes years of historical performance data to achieve "near-perfect*

*information"* as well as human expertise and critical thinking to define what makes a *"great"* customer support representative or engineer. Hence, today's organizations will benefit in the majority of cases from utilizing a combination of data science and human expertise. It is preferable over a computers-only or humans-only approach, both of which will provide biased and likely inaccurate predictions.

Authors: How should companies prioritize AI projects? How are you doing it?

*Danilo: AI is only a tool, and often a tool that is best used in combination with human expertise. It should not be thought of as a replacement for critical strategic thinking. Teams that perform time-consuming, repetitive, or error-prone tasks should evaluate whether technology can augment their business processes and, if so, roll it out gradually to stay in control. This is how we work with our customers, often starting with paid pilots or smaller rollouts in controlled environments. If the results are satisfactory, the executive should be able to make a business case for the solution and minimize risk for both themselves and their CFO.*

Authors: What are some of the best practices you've seen with regard to AI in the workplace?

*Danilo: Approach solutions and vendors that claim AI with a healthy mix of optimism and skepticism. [Some of our early customers are already generating millions of dollars of value and savings thanks to their investment in our solution. However, they got there by evaluating different vendors thoughtfully and making a case for the solution and need before backing the initiative with large budgets.] Organizations should approach AI-powered solutions with the same mindset as they would any other strategic initiative. Make the business case by evaluating the benefits, required investment and risks thoughtfully, pilot the technology in a controlled environment, and follow best practices to gradually deploy the solution at scale.*

Authors: Companies are part of an economic ecosystem including various stakeholders such as other companies, government, academia, and others. What role do stakeholders need to play to help AI flourish in companies?

*Danilo: We try to set the example at our organization by operating on three principles:*
*1. We collaborate with regulatory authorities to ensure we are compliant and help inform them on technological changes they may not be equipped to predict.*
*2. We collaborate with academia, specifically the Purdue University I/O Psychology lab ran by Dr. Louis Tay, where we validate the technology and investigate its potential weaknesses to address them before it is put in the hand of any customer.*

> 3. *Finally, we partner with our customers to ensure they follow and share best practices to enjoy the benefits of these breakthrough technologies without compliance or privacy risks.*
>
> Authors: What do you think are essential leadership attributes in the AI revolution? Why?
>
> *Danilo: In line with best practices we discussed earlier, I think it is the job of the modern leader to keep herself informed and be aware of both the benefits and the potential risks that technology can provide. Failing at either of those will lead their organization to fall behind the competition or, alternatively, face major legal or PR risk.*
>
> Authors: What do you think is the future of AI in the workplace? How will work be transformed?
>
> *Danilo: I believe the future of AI in the workplace will be "augmented intelligence," not "artificial intelligence." As operators on the cutting edge of the industry, working hand in hand with the most innovative Fortune 500 organizations, we are intimately aware of the potential and the shortcomings of technology. If these experiences have taught me anything, it is that technology as powerful as AI is only as effective as those implementing it.*

Quote-investigation focuses on exploring the origins of a quote. Fortunately, there is a site named quoteinvestigator.com that provides history of quotes. One of the quotes explored is the age-old "Give a man a fish, and you feed him for a day. Teach a man to fish, and you feed him for a lifetime." Quote investigator investigated the history of the quote and found the following excerpt from the twelfth-century philosopher Maimonides when he wrote about eight degrees in the duty of charity:

> In 1826 an explication of the eighth degree was published in a journal called "The Religious Intelligencer." (Quoteinvestigator, 2018)
>
> Lastly, the eighth and the most meritorious of all, is to anticipate charity by preventing poverty, namely, to assist the reduced brother, either by a considerable gift or loan of money, or by teaching him a trade, or by putting him in the way of business, so that he may earn an honest livelihood and not be forced to the dreadful alternative of holding up his hand for charity.

Thus, the recognition that teaching how to fish is far more efficient, and of course noble action than simply giving the fish to someone is as powerful of a lesson in charity as it is in ML.

Teaching computers to perform tasks by giving specific instructions one by one is known as programming. Programming has done wonders for us. Almost all the major applications used prior to the cognitive revolution were a product of programming. From enterprise resource planning systems to customer relationship management systems, all were built by programming. But in programming, you must provide step-by-step instructions to a computer. Now, even to do a small thinking task, this can get very complicated quickly. Fortunately, there is another way around: teaching the computer how to fish instead of giving the fish. This means teaching computers how to do tasks by learning.

Thus, ML can be viewed as techniques designed to teach computers such that they can learn on their own. An example will clarify. Let us say you are tired of receiving spam and you want to build a system to identify and place spam in your junk mail. The programming way to do that will be to create a file that will have e-mails of all your legitimate e-mail senders (e.g., family, friend, business) and another file of spam e-mailers. Every time you would get a new good e-mail, you will add the sender to your contacts list and when a new bad e-mail comes you will add the sender to your spam file. Next time when the sender sends you an e-mail, the program will look for if the e-mail sender is in the good list or bad list and based upon that determination it will send the e-mail to your inbox or to the junk mail. If it found the sender in neither category, it will send you the e-mail in your inbox, so you can classify it manually. As you can tell, life will become quite difficult if you are constantly classifying hundreds—even thousands—of new junk e-mails that originate daily from millions of junk senders around the world. Thus, programming does not appear to be an efficient way to solve this problem.

> LEADERSHIP INSIGHT 5: ML is teaching machines how to seek solutions to problems without giving them specific line-by-line instructions. Programming-centric information technology, in which one provides line-by-line instructions, is different from ML. Leaders need to take this into account in their operations.

Teaching how to fish is another option. In this, you can teach the machine to do the job for you. How can you do that? When you teach, you help students learn general concepts such that students can formalize and apply the specifics.

When we learn about things in our world, we learn how to generalize things. For example, if I were learning what a car is, I can develop a general concept of a car (shape, four tires, steering wheel, doors, etc.) and apply that concept to figure out that Mini and Prius are cars and so are Lincoln and a limousine—even though a limousine may look much bigger and different than a Mini. For the same reason a child can identify a toy car as a car. Thus, we are not learning the specifics, but instead our power to learn lies in learning the general aspects or features of things. Once we acquire that understanding, then we apply it to determine the specifics. This is exactly how machines learn.

Going back to the e-mail example, to teach machines the general aspect or features of what bad e-mails versus good e-mail could be is an important part of teaching how to distinguish between good and bad e-mails. Let us say we identify features such as the sender has been sending e-mails in the past, that you have responded to the e-mails via reply or forward, that the sender's e-mail appears to be from a well-known firm, that the e-mail content does not contain typical spam words, that the e-mail was addressed to you—these are the examples of what constitute as features. Based upon these features, now you can teach a machine to classify suspicious e-mails as junk or good. Obviously, machine may make some mistakes when performing this function and you may find some of your good e-mails were classified as junk or vice versa, but as soon as you tell the machine the right classification, it learns more about your preferences and becomes better in classifying. By teaching the machine to fish, you now have given it the power to become intelligent on accomplishing a task.

Unlike you, who needs to worry about paying college tuition, losing weight, picking up kids from school, or asking for a raise from a difficult boss, the life of a smart classifying engine is pretty simple. It only has to worry about classifying e-mails and hence it can become very good at solving this problem. In its "narrow" function, it will continue to learn and improve and become the best classifier saving you hours and headache of classifying junk e-mails.

Thus, teaching to fish is a far superior way than giving the fish. By helping computers to learn for themselves, we have created a breakthrough and this breakthrough is driving a lot of what is transpiring today.

## BROAD TYPES OF ML

ML is the part of AI in which algorithms are trained with data to teach machines how to perform cognitive functions. For example, machines can spot trends, understand similar or related objects, make predictions, classify items, and discover patterns.

Think of it as finding a mathematical function or link between data in which we know the $x$ or input values and two or more $y$ or output values. Since we know the right answers and wrong answers, we can teach the machine to identify the relationship between the data inputs and outputs. For example, we can teach the machine to recognize that a certain combination of words (input) represents good feelings versus bad feelings (output). This type of training is known as supervised learning. In supervised learning, we provide labeled data to machines to help them understand the right versus wrong answers. Based upon their training, they learn how to generalize and apply that learning to solve problems that they have not seen before.

In some cases, however, we may not have labeled data. The problem could be that we may not even know what we are looking for. In this problem area we are, trying to identify patterns based upon inputs only and without any output information. Unlike supervised learning where we feed the computer both input data and the output data as labels, we don't have any labeled data, so we only feed the input data to the machine. In this case, our hope is that the machine can help us identify patterns of data based upon proximity or closeness to each other. We assume that data that relates to potential outputs (which may be new concepts) will cluster together and hence allow us to observe some new patterns. This is known as unsupervised learning.

Another way to teach machines is to let them learn on their own by making mistakes and correcting their course. To facilitate that type of learning in which a robot can learn on its own by trial and error, we need to provide guidance in terms of what constitutes as success. A special kind of learning known as reinforcement learning is employed where a reward function is established for success. In 1951, Marvin Minsky of MIT conducted an experiment in which he created an artificial rat that moved through a maze and the mouse learned the moves such that its performance improved with every successful outcome. It was a simple deployment of reinforcement learning where the rat's synaptic connections would strengthen every time it successfully exited the maze.

## ALGORITHMS AND DATA

You need two things to train a machine: lots of data and algorithms. Large amounts of data are needed so the machine can use that to learn and to predict. The role of algorithm is to find the most optimized and refined model of learning. When machines learn, they can be all over the place. What algorithms do is to bring them closer and closer to the right answer. Once the right answer is learned, when new inputs are given to the machine, it can acquire the ability to generalize learning and give intelligent results. Many types of learning techniques are used including deep learning, clustering, reinforcement learning, decision tree learning, inductive logic programming, and Bayesian networks.

Pedro Domingos (2015) in his landmark book *The Master Algorithm* divides ML into five tribes of symbolists, connectionists, evolutionists, bayesians, and analogizers. Below, we will discuss a recent model that came out of the connectionist tribe and that has gained significant popularity.

## DEEP DOWN IN THE CONSCIOUSNESS OF BEING

Artificial neural networks come from the connectionist tribe and they are patterned after the human brain. Just as we have neurons, neural networks try to replicate our mental processing and are inspired by biological brains. In an artificial network, however, since we are not dealing with a biological brain, we need to make some adjustments to be able to replicate the behavior. So, we establish layers in which artificial neurons reside, form connections between the neurons, and enable directions in which data propagates. So, when a neuron gets an input, it assigns a weight to it—and then passes it on to another neuron in the next layer. The receiving neuron does the same thing and passes it to on the next, and this goes on until the last layer that gives out the output. The output is compared to the right or known answer, and then, based upon the distance between the correct answer and the result reported by the network, feedback is sent through the networks backward—a process known as back propagation. The purpose of the feedback is to readjust the weights so that to nudge the network to come close to the right answer. The process continues until the distance between the right answers and the network-generated answers is minimized.

For example, if you feed an image of a human and the machine is trying to determine if it is a human, the machine will first have to learn what humans look like.

To teach a machine what humans look like, we establish a network composed of several layers of neurons. A neural network can have many layers. The layer through which the inputs are fed into the network is known as the input layer and the layer through which the network produces the output is known as the output layer. Other layers, known as the hidden layers, are in between the input and the output layers. We start feeding this network images of humans and nonhumans where each image is broken down into very small fragments, like tiny tiles, converted into numbers, and then fed into the network. As neurons from the first layer receive the input, weights are assigned to each piece of input and the adjusted product of weights and the initial input is passed on to the neurons in the subsequent layer. The neurons in the subsequent layer again assign the weights to the incoming input and pass it on to the next layer as output and so on. Once the results reach the last layer, also known as the output layer, the output is compared to the right answer.

Based upon the output, a probability vector is produced that signifies how confident the machine is in terms of its answer about the image. Since we already know the right answer, we can tell the machine the difference between machine's answer and the right answer. Using that feedback, the machine then adjusts the weights assigned and keeps going through the process to reduce its error in identifying humans.

For example, in this case the right answer is whether the picture is of a human or not. A machine may suggest an answer, but the job of this step is to understand the distance or differential between the right answer (i.e., the answer that is known to us) to the answer being proposed by the machine. Once the machine understands that difference, it attempts to go back and readjust the weights. After readjusting the weights, it tries to make another pass at it and then once again identifies the distance between the right answer and that proposed by the machine and gives feedback to the network which once again readjusts the weights. This process continues and repeats itself multiple times and finally the machine minimizes the distance between the right answer and the wrong answer. That's when the machine has learned how to do a task. This whole process in which you teach a machine when you already know the right answers is known as supervised learning and the model you used is known as neural network or deep learning.

As more and more data are fed to it and it understands the image features that make a human, its understanding of what humans look like becomes better. It does that by tweaking the weights of the neurons. And then, once trained, it can learn to spot a human from an image based upon the above technique.

With the growth of processing power via advanced graphics processing units (GPUs), it became possible to build a large number of hidden layers in a neural network and this became deep neural networks. With large number of neurons and deep layers, these networks became powerful enough to perform sophisticated learning functions such as image, video, and voice analysis.

## REINFORCEMENT AND DEEP LEARNING COMBINED

While an image-recognizing algorithm can be fed as millions of images for it to learn, such a method may not be feasible for training robots or for solving complex problems or learning games where the number of possibilities exceed the ability of a computer to process in terms of discrete game moves. When images are fed as data for learning purposes, human guidance about what constitutes as correct answers is provided. Since an image constitutes a limited number of possibilities, that guidance is less complex when compared to the world of possibilities for a robot or a game environment. To train such systems one needs to recognize that they operate in a complex space where the number of possibilities are enormous.

Limited by processing power and the methodology deployed, reinforcement learning remained underutilized up until the point when it was realized that deep learning can be used to process and update large amounts of data needed to make reinforcement learning a success in more complex applications. The AlphaGo story told in Chapter 1 of the book is also an example of successful deployment of reinforcement learning—and so are autonomous cars and advanced robots. Robots can be trained by having them observe humans, by trial and error, by kinesthetic (i.e., helping a robot perform a task), and by remote control.

But neither reinforcement learning, nor deep learning neural networks alone could have accomplished the amazing feat of the AlphaGo's repeated victories. It was the combination of the two that created the spark that made the magic happen. As David Silver, a member of the visionary AlphaGo team, explained, it was the marriage of the two that created the AI revolution (Silver et al., 2017).

The power of digital bots and robots is being used to transform modern companies. Innovation and progress in this area are at an irreversible path. If anything, executives should expect more, and not less of these remarkable and transformative technologies to play a bigger and more important role in the workplace.

From a corporate perspective, two types of technologies are finding wide adoption:

## ROBOTIC PROCESS AUTOMATION—THE OTHER AUTOMATION

Robotic Process Automation (RPA) is the automation of typical clerical tasks such as data entry. RPA implementation involves automating the tasks that are typically low variability, repeatable, tasks that are performed by humans and that require low cognitive ability. It can be viewed as the digital or virtual parallel of a basic low intelligence mechanical or physical robot. Some argue that since there is no learning embedded in RPA, the solution is not AI. This, however, does not diminish the role of RPA as it can help a lot in building the automation platform for full-scale automation.

RPA can enable the automation of many such processes that need to be automated and where ML will be an overkill.

## THE DO, THINK, DEVELOP MODEL

Automation has three types Do, Think, and Develop. You can view them as three types of machines.

**The *Do* Automation:** The most straightforward application of AI is to automate the repeatable, low intelligence parts of existing processes. This means to study the monotonous, low variability, repeatable existing process – such as data reconciliation – and then automating it by deploying RPA technology. These are simple processes or parts of processes, such as updating a form or making calculations, and they can be automated by robotic process automation.

**The *Think* Automation:** More complex processes that require decision-making, learning, and experience can be automated via ML. ML can automate more complex current processes that require specialized human thinking and decision-making and it can also create or extend new processes that don't exist at present. AI can be used to enhance the current processes by adding new dimensions or extensions. An example will be the ability of a retailer to study the historical buying patterns in sales as well as the behavior of the customer to make recommendations with a high likelihood of sales potential. Such a recommendation engine may not be part of the original sales process, but the sales process has been extended to include this. Note that this is more than simply getting insights from data, as this includes incorporating insights into actions and doing that in real time.

**The *Develop* Automation:** AI can help develop or accelerate the development of new ideas, research, products, business models, and insights. AI can be deployed to augment current business models or to develop completely new ones. AI can provide the insights that augment the ability of the executives and organizations to develop a higher state of awareness. For example, pharmaceutical companies are using AI to develop new molecules to develop new drugs.

LEADERSHIP INSIGHT 6: There are three types of work that are being automated and leaders need to weigh upon them:

- The Do Automation
- The Think Automation
- The Develop Automation

In the featured interview in the beginning of the chapter, Raphael Danilo said, "AI is only a tool, and often a tool that is best used in combination with human expertise." With the expanded growth in AI usage and multitude of technology tools in workplaces around the world, leaders are empowered to tame machines and optimize operational performance.

CHAPTER 4

# THE THREE STATES OF AN AI LEADER

*If your actions inspire others to dream more, learn more, do more and become more, you are a leader.*

—JOHN QUINCY ADAMS

---

**EXECUTIVE INTERVIEW 4**

**Chris Platts, Cofounder and CEO, ThriveMap**

Authors: How would you describe the current state of artificial intelligence (AI) in your industry?

*Platts: In the recruitment technology sector, I'd say that, in a lot of areas, the marketing is ahead of the science. There's no true AI in recruiting just yet— although a lot of vendors will use the word. There are some helpful tools that use machine learning algorithms and the best use of this technology is in automating predictable tasks such as onboarding, scheduling, and candidate sourcing. When it comes to using AI to automate complex decisions such as who to hire, I'm yet to see any evidence that it leads to better outcomes whilst also being fair for candidates. The issue with biased datasets being reinforced by AI still prevails.*

Authors: In what way has AI transformed your organization?

*Platts: We're a small, distributed organization that creates personalized pre-hire assessments for volume hiring. We don't use AI in our scoring systems because we believe that hiring decisions should be fully transparent. Companies should be able to explain how a recruitment decision was reached or they're at risk of litigation and true AI systems typically can't provide that.*

Authors: How is AI creating value for your firm?

*Platts:* We're presently exploring the utility of machine learning to automate the process of analyzing correlations between how employees perform on their pre-employment assessments and how they perform as employees in the role. This is something we do anyway, but through automation, we can provide real-time suggestions to our partner companies on how they can improve the predictive validity of their assessments over time.

Authors: What do you think are current organizational challenges relating to AI?

*Platts:* In the domain of using AI to augment business intelligence, I think the primary challenge is being able to explain how decisions are reached. When dealing with people decisions such as who to promote or who to hire, we know that human decision-making is biased, we can create processes to minimize bias, but you can never eliminate it. AI faces the same challenges as we do in this field because the data it gets is inherently biased. If we can solve for this, then it opens up exciting fields of innovation.

Authors: What is not being done right in the AI revolution?

*Platts:* I think AI as a term has suffered from concept creep; it's become so big and amorphous that it risks becoming largely irrelevant. It feels like when we can't be bothered to actually explain the solution we label it as AI and everyone nods their head in agreement. It's lazy thinking and it leads to lousy outcomes.

Authors: Where do you think opportunities exist with regard to AI in the workplace?

*Platts:* Any areas where the primary business need revolves around saving time. Getting business insight and intelligence can be incredibly useful but of course, but how much of this is down to true AI is debatable—it depends on your own definition of what is true AI at work.

Authors: In your opinion, what should and what should not be automated? Why?

*Platts:* It's probably wrong to create a blanket mantra here but typically I find that anything manual, repetitive, and low-skilled that takes considerable time should be automated, whereas anything complex, nuanced should not be automated; instead, technology can be used to augment not replace human judgment.

Authors: How should companies prioritize AI projects? How are you doing it?

*Platts:* I'd suggest starting with the biggest business needs listed in order of priority, once you have the list you need to judge which ones are efficiency related and rank these in order of the amount of time saved if that process could be partially or fully automated using AI.

Authors: What are some of the best practices you've seen with regard to AI in the workplace?

*Platts: I think the simple things that we do every day have the greatest impact on business productivity. Such as suggesting words and phrases before you type them, e-mail spam filters, and automatic calendar scheduling. I have a friend that's starting a company that automatically transcribes job interviews, scores candidates, and spots bias from interviewers. That's a pretty neat idea, but from what I've seen we're still not there yet in terms of execution.*

Authors: Companies are part of an economic ecosystem including various stakeholders such as other companies, government, academia, and others. What role do stakeholders need to play to help AI flourish in companies?

*Platts: I think a clearer definition and language to use around AI would be helpful. The more precise we are with our language around the type of intelligence being performed the more confidence companies will have in implementing a solution. That definition should come from academia, but be supported by governments and companies. Ultimately it's about trust and evidence. The more we can evidence AI making a difference to business performance the more people will use it.*

Authors: What do you think are essential leadership attributes in the AI revolution? Why?

*Platts: I think it depends on the type of organization you are today, but more importantly who you want to be tomorrow. Every company will use AI in different ways, so it's too general to say certain traits or attributes should be valued over others.*

Authors: What do you think is the future of AI in the workplace? How will work be transformed?

*Platts: There's huge scope for AI to improve our daily lives at work from smart assistants that offer support as well as just scheduling to intuitive voice to text transcription to save us from needing to write e-mails or documents. My hope is that AI delivers time back to people in order to create new opportunities to really connect with each other. My fear is that companies will just keep raising their expectations of business productivity and we reallocate the time we've saved using AI solutions back into working harder and achieving more than ever before. So essentially I predict that everything will change and nothing will change.*

The existing theory of leadership was developed for the antiquated twentieth-century model of leadership and management. The advent of AI is requiring the development of new theoretical frameworks for leadership. The magnitude of change forces us to make substantial changes in the existing theoretical models to or even propose new models that can address this emerging transformation.

Studying leadership has become somewhat like astrology. Dozens of definitions, hypotheticals, models, and arbitrary approaches continue to tempt our imagination. Thus, business leadership often leaves the universe of science and assumes the mysterious essence of religion. Leadership lessons are derived from unexplainable attachments, emotional idealizations, unconditional devotions, charisma, celebrity worship, memes, and apotheosis-like glorification. Like religious zeolites, business researchers try to use pseudoscience instead of data and facts. While this apophatic tendency to compromise on facts often results in a deeply satisfying comfort of feeding our confirmation bias and provides a compelling platform to sell books and consulting services, it doesn't give us the scientific basis to develop a reliable theory of business leadership.

The real craft happens when leadership gurus try to force fit better performing companies with arbitrarily or randomly developed leadership qualities and explanations. Since randomness dictates that at least some of those coincidences will be possible, companies with superior results are automatically linked with subjective leadership models.

These types of pseudoscientific theories of leadership are often marketed, sold as panacea for all ills that haunt companies, branded as easy-to-learn magic bullet solutions, labeled for wide consumption, and sold as popular literature in business. With a plethora of vocabulary describing various leadership models—for instance, charismatic, transactional, transformational, servant, and the like—leadership business has become a major seller.

It is likely that the advent of AI will nullify such subjective leadership and management science adventures. We believe that a passion for objectivity, ethics, data orientation, and empathy will be necessary for the modern-day AI leaders.

When major technological revolutions happen, leaders must readjust strategies and manage the implementation of strategies differently. When the industrial revolution gave way to the information or knowledge revolution, leaders adapted. Focusing on information processing machines became just as important as focusing on industrial-era manufacturing machines.

Similarly, as we transition to the cognitive era, moving from information technology (IT) to cognitive technologies will be critical. This implies that leading organizations through a massive change process requires how leaders approach technology but also how they approach leadership. It changes how leaders relate and interact with followers and how they view themselves. It also adds a new dimension of responsibility.

This chapter focuses on understanding how to build leaders for the AI revolution.

## THE AUTOMATION LEADER

The CEO, CFO, COO, CMO, or any other senior executive seeking to become an automation leader has three key leadership sides:

- Lead the Transformation: In this area she leads her firm from low-intelligence automation to high-intelligence automation. She does it effectively. This means she avoids waste, misadventures, and overinvestment and achieves results such that her firm's competitive advantage is secured. Thus, performance in the cognitive transformation can be divided into two simultaneous and equally desirable pursuits. The first pursuit includes factors such as what leaders need to do to stay competitive, how should they approach the technological transformation, and how they must incorporate AI in their overall strategy and execution plans. This is State 1 Leadership and the tools to achieve State 1 Leadership are discussed in this chapter and in Chapter 5.
- Lead Ethics: In this area she ensures that the products, services, and the operating infrastructure used to support products and services do not violate ethics. She ensures that AI artifacts are not used to manipulate or exploit customers or other stakeholders, that human rights and climate are protected, and that social interests are upheld. The second pursuit focuses on understanding the governance and ethical needs of participating and building value for the human civilization. This is known as State 2 Leadership and the tools to achieve success are discussed in this chapter and in Chapter 6.
- Develop New Personal Leadership Qualities: The mindset shaped to lead a twentieth-century organization is not necessarily, or easily, transportable to modern-day AI-centric organization. A leader has to develop new skills and some of those are discussed in this chapter. For example, machines, if developed right, will provide extremely objective and decision-relevant information. In areas in which human decision-making and actions will follow the analysis provided by AI, leaders of the future will have to learn to trust the AI. At times, the AI analysis will go counter to the human gut feeling, but objectivity often appears at

odds with our biases. In this state, a leader is self-aware of who she is as a human and becomes keenly aware of her values. This is known as State 3 Leadership.

## STATE 1 LEADERSHIP: BUSINESS CONTEXT

State 1 refers to creating super-powerful business results by deploying AI-centric business transformation. When the Internet revolution unfolded and if you were Blockbuster Video, it was not enough for you to compete in your traditional business model of operating physical stores. You also needed to simultaneously evolve to face the emerging realities of challenge posed by innovators like Netflix. This dual management of managing the *today*, while working on the *tomorrow*, becomes extremely hard.

In some ways, it is easy for new innovators to focus on the tomorrow, since they don't have to worry about the today. Legacy businesses do. Hence one of the biggest challenges for business leaders is to successfully transform their current business to a modern cognitive business. Moving from the info-industrial era to the cognitive era will require true leadership.

If you look at it from an executive's perspective: what are her choices? If she doesn't adopt AI, her business interests will get impacted, her firm will fall behind, her competitors will gain an edge, and sooner or later her company will get crushed by the rise of the advanced technology by her competitors.

As the cognitive era unfolds, the leadership challenge is simple: adapt or get annihilated. The previous sentence is not delivered to create fear. It is also not the intention of the authors to shock their readers with sensational statements. It is there because the authors firmly believe that if AI paradigm is not understood and applied by modern-day leaders, there is a real risk to business, society, and economy. When the Internet revolution transpired, the changing economic dynamics were unforgiving, and the same will be true in the AI revolution.

AI is the competitive advantage and a necessary part of business strategy. This means that AI will rapidly grow, get funded, and will be deployed in all areas of business.

AI's relentless and unstoppable growth is a reality that our civilization must face. This reality however implies that the burden of governing AI resides with the business and government leaders. It also means that business and government leaders should take this change extremely seriously and should not be mesmerized by the glamor. It means having critics is a good thing and we need more of those—just as we need more data scientists and AI experts.

## All Strategy Needs to Be About AI

First, integrate AI in the firm's strategic planning such that the first question that must be answered is: How can AI be a source of competitive advantage for the firm and what business model changes are forthcoming or needed? This means to integrate AI in day-to-day operations of a firm—for example, in the functional areas of marketing, finance, sales, operations, supply chain management, human resources, and the like.

Leaders need to understand the possibilities associated with cognitive transformation. This means that all business decisions, all capital investment, all processes, all functional areas, all strategic plans, and all business models need to be reanalyzed from the cognitive angle. It is critical to explore what possibilities exist with AI and how AI will support or even take over decision-making.

## Build Strong AI-Centric Transformation Programs

Cognitive-era leaders must launch powerful programs to build the technological transformation. They must prepare their employees and other stakeholders. They must incorporate the cognitive transformation in their business plans and allocate capital. They must develop and analyze new business models in accordance with the opportunity provided by technology. All of those skills require a good understanding of both technical possibilities and business. Most importantly, being able to think business processes and models from a different perspective will be critical.

For example, Amazon's leadership has declared that they are building a company around AI—a concept they call "the flywheel." What is your firm's flywheel?

## AI Is Not IT, A Good Automation Leader Understands That

Cognitive-era leaders need to reorient themselves from non-intelligent information to intelligent IT. The regular early twenty-first-century Internet centric digital transformation is not AI-based transformation. Intelligent automation requires systems to automate skilled work performed by humans. Recall the three types of systems from the previous chapter—the Do automation, the Think automation, and the Develop automation. What separates intelligent automation from regular IT is that intelligent systems are based upon machine learning and not programming. Unless specifically trained on AI, regular programmers, system designers, and even CIO/CTO are not AI people. AI resources typically come from data science and AI backgrounds. Also, data management is different than data science. Firms may need to create new departments to lead the AI transformation.

## *Define Problems Differently*

Australia's largest independent oil and gas company Woodside Energy was facing a major business problem. As experienced employees were retiring, the company needed not only to capture their knowledge and experience but also to apply it to provide real-time information to new hires and less-experienced employees. This meant that Woodside needed to have information on its highly complex oil exploration structures built in remote parts of ocean. Woodside implemented IBM Watson by feeding it information and training it as an engineer. Once done, the system became the go-to engineer to ask questions. By having such large sets of information processed through cognitive engines, the company reported that it could see things that it didn't know before.

The important factors to understand here are that the leaders of Woodside Energy understood that the solution to retiring employees was not hiring more employees to cross-train or recording information in a noncognitive knowledge domains. They recognized that the optimum solution is to rely upon the most modern and advanced technology based upon AI.

For example, the operational leaders of Woodside Energy would have needed a different state of awareness to understand the role and power of the IBM Watson solution. They would have needed the ability to analyze their problem with a different mindset. Being able to analyze existing problems and standard solutions with a nonstandard and innovative mindset requires bold leadership.

## *Operate with a Plan*

AI leaders must have a clear and pragmatic plan to lead the transformation. Whether achieved by creating a new department or a center of excellence, the plan should include all departments and a full transformation of business. This department should directly report to the CEO and should be viewed as a new type of COO role.

## *Move to a Centralized Planning Model*

Currently companies are using a decentralized automation model where each department is pursuing independent intelligent automation. Departments are being guided by consulting firms and vendors, and executives are operating with their own agendas and viewpoints. Firms need an integrated automation strategy and this is where centralized planning becomes necessary.

**STATE 2 LEADERSHIP: STRATEGIC OWNERSHIP**

State 2 Leadership means one must ensure that ethics are integrated with the business strategy. Leaders who will build companies based upon State 1 Leadership may achieve success, but such a success will be short-lived. A State 2 Leader fully understand the impact of AI on society, employees, economy, human civilization, politics, human potential, environment, and other such areas. The ethics and governance side of AI must go hand in hand with the business success.

## *Understand the Risks of AI*

AI leaders need to be highly ethical and visionary. More than anything else, they need to embrace and understand the impact on human civilization as the world makes the cognitive transition. This means leaders need to retrain themselves on ethical considerations and dilemmas. Great minds such as Bill Gates, Stephen Hawking, and Elon Musk have warned us about the risks of AI. While such warnings are being issued from extraordinarily smart and accomplished people, they are being viewed as media sound bites and memes. They are not being taken seriously. If the same three people or people with similar influence issued a warning that a financial market crash is imminent or that a meteoroid is heading our way, people will pay attention. Executives will put in place teams to prepare for the impact. Financial markets would incorporate risk. Policy makers will become vigilant. But when it comes to AI, we tend to view their warnings as media hype.

Humans have very little experience with autonomous technologies. This implies that there could be significant risk in making the transition. As autonomous cars appear on highways and healthcare robots become part of the workforce, leaders should understand the legal implications as well as the potential risk. In the new environment crisis management should be given a high priority.

## *Remove the Bias*

The most important challenge will be to understand the ethical and governance challenges and understand them in an unbiased manner. Such bias exists both at a strategic level and at the product level. For example, while congress and the White House have both tried to understand the ethical and governance issues of technology, both tend to receive and rely upon information either from large tech firms (Google, Facebook, etc.) or from institutions that are either funded by large tech firms (Google, Facebook, etc.) or tech executives and entrepreneurs who have significant investments in AI. Clearly, there is a conflict of interest issue when ethics and governance information is received from these firms. This is the strategic bias.

Product bias comes from embedding biased data into products such that AI artifacts learn to be biased.

### *Learn about the Technology*

Leaders should also learn about the governance and ethical issues of implementing autonomous or AI systems from independent sources.

The technology is relatively new and the awareness about the possibilities is still in infancy stages. In many cases, companies are making decisions to pursue new projects and make operational decisions without truly understanding the potential of AI.

## STATE 3 LEADERSHIP: STAKEHOLDER RESPONSIBILITY

A self-aware leader not only understands how to ethically create business value from automation but also possesses a deeper insight about himself or herself. The State 3 Leader must develop new skills that were not part of the previous leadership models.

### *Reliance on Decisions by Machines*

As shown in the book (which later also became a movie) *Moneyball: The Art of Winning an Unfair Game*, data-centric decision-making can often be counter intuitive. With more automation, leaders will have to develop new skills to rely on data and fight their own instincts to make decisions based upon their subjective opinions.

Leaders would need to develop skills to rely upon objective information provided by AI. This means that they would learn to overcome their own biases. In business where leadership is often viewed as one based upon traits, charisma, and gut feel, this could be a new learning for leaders. They need to develop greater comfort and reliance on decisions made by the AI systems. Leadership will eventually become shared leadership with machine. This will not mean that machines will be dictating their terms. It simply means that many functions of leadership will be taken over by machines.

## *Recognize That AI Will Be Analyzing Your Leadership Style*

Business, as we know it today, is a relatively new phenomenon. Politics, bureaucracy, military, and even sports predate modern business. Thus, it is natural for business researchers to study leadership in other domains and to use those frameworks as the baseline to develop new theories of leadership. This creates a confusing cocktail factor. The cocktail factor is approaching political, military, sports, and business leadership as if they are all the same.

This typical jumbled variety of leadership models is both misleading and problematic. It makes no distinction between different types of leadership challenges. There is little evidence that leaders from military, politics, or sports make good business leaders—or for that matter good business leaders make great political or military leaders.

Since both the goals and stakeholders vary across different kinds of leaders, AI will help draw a clear line of demarcation between business leaders and others. In fact, before even selecting top leaders, AI may help create an objective leadership profile that will highlight the most promising leaders of the future. To select future leaders, boards may use that analysis as doctors use radiology reports.

Such leadership profiles are being developed as machines scan information about leaders, their decisions, and their communications. From annual filings to earnings calls and conference speeches to interviews, data is being used to analyze the leadership and management styles of leaders. The obvious question remains: Is it ethical to develop such profiles?

## *Self-Awareness Means to Learn to Focus on Value Creation*

The AI revolution will force leaders to focus more on value creation activities—such as innovation and new business model development. Most importantly, leaders need to encourage their AI experts to minimize or eliminate human bias from being transferred into AI.

In many cases, leaders arise from random events. Oftentimes, being at the right time and right place gives leaders their distinguished status. Followers are often attracted and mobilized by the power of the glamor appeal and not some objective criteria. Hence, the image of leadership congeals via a snowball-like self-fulfilling prophecy. And when leaders become the fortunate beneficiaries of randomness, whether they influenced the business results or not, theorists comb through the traits of leaders and form theories of leadership. This process could be highly vulnerable to subjective assessment and value judgment and it turns the undeserving into legends.

It must be recognized that leaders will now be leading human and digital workers. That means that leaders today are responsible for both human and digital workers.

Leaders have to now develop skills to communicate the transformation, the value impact, and the power of such solutions.

When machines are part of the workforce, would the traditional traits such as how leaders communicate, interact, or motivate change? What would the change look like? Leaders will need to develop new skills to communicate and use modern tools to understand how to optimize communications.

More than anything else we believe that objectivity, diversity in educational background, ethics, and empathy will be the driving forces of determining future leaders.

### *Leaders Can Garner the Power of AI to Communicate Better*

Scholars generally tend to agree that as a common denominator, leadership has something to do with "influence"—as in influencing others to voluntarily agree with the vision of the leader and then to mobilize the followers to achieve that vision. In many cases, what leaders do with that influence was considered irrelevant or unimportant. Thus, whether leaders use their influence to save humanity or conduct a genocide was often ignored as a variable.

In a world defined by autonomous bots having the power to influence presidential elections, start revolutions, social media creating viral videos daily, information overload, and the ability to observe and influence human behavior at a deep physiological level, "influence" can no longer be just tied to human-centered leadership. Machines can be used to acquire undue influence.

### *Management Approaches Are Significant*

Returning to the business leadership concept, perhaps nothing offends businesspeople more than being called managers when the title of a "leader" can be bestowed upon them. This disdain of managers reveals the bigotry of leadership romanticism in which leader's "being-ness" is artfully separated from leader's achievements. Thus, a great deal of literature is devoted to articulating the difference between leaders and managers (Collier 1978; Bertocci 2009; Edwards 2015). This status segregation may be another instrument of widely prevalent idealization in leadership studies—and perhaps a result of the inability to separate other types of leaderships from business leadership. In business, management and leadership are often required to be simultaneously present traits, so integrated, that their coexistence is the only proof of the performance excellence of any one of the traits individually. This interdependence means that one cannot exist without the other.

Since AI economy will require leaders to perform against highly competitive standards, management will become leadership and leadership will become management. What about influence?

For many decades, the influence factor was considered sufficient to join the leaders' club. In recent decades, some researchers made a case for qualifying leaders based on "values" and not just influence. While adding values to the leadership equation was a noble move, researchers completely ignored the distinction between different types of leadership. Once again, such comparisons tend to shift the limelight away from business leadership in favor of political and military leaderships.

In one manifestation of the influence-based conceptualization, leadership is also viewed as an active relationship that exists between leaders and their followers. Some argue that followers can have influence of their own (Rost 1993). The rise of retail investor class and ESG (environment, social, governance) activism indicates that masses can garner new power and influence.

AI is about to show us what real leadership is all about. It will link leadership with true results and it will be primarily driven by empathy.

> LEADERSHIP INSIGHT 7: There are three levels of leadership needed to win in the AI revolution:
>
> State 1 Leadership: Business value focused to successfully lead firms through the great transformation.
> State 2 Leadership: In addition to State 1, leaders apply and maintain higher level of ethics in all parts of their transformational strategy.
> State 3 Leadership: Leaders develop a deeper sense of who they are, develop greater self-awareness, and focus on stakeholder betterment.

## AI WILL DEFINE LEADERSHIP AS ONE THAT FILLS THE COGNITIVE VOID

To describe one type of leadership, some scholars have argued that leadership is not individualistic or person based—it stems from the unison of many and as a shared role, and such a leadership model is based upon tenets such as "concurrent, collective, collaborative, and compassionate" (Raelin 2003). This implies that multiple leaders can operate simultaneously, and decisions are made by whoever has the relevant responsibility. Even though such thinking was probably driven by egalitarian concerns, particularly as a modernist rebellion against self-serving hierarchical structures, this model appears to be more business friendly. But still this model doesn't go far enough to provide a business-centric definition of leadership—and continues to link leadership with influence.

In the AI world, business leadership will find a new definition and would likely emerge as follows: Business leadership is making good decisions under uncertainty and driving business results that help advance and progress human civilization forward and improve human life. As Chris Platts mentioned in the chapter interview, *"ultimately, it's about trust and evidence."* Business leadership will be viewed as one that fills the human cognitive void and focuses on the benefit of humankind.

CHAPTER 5

# STATE 1 LEADERSHIP: BUSINESS CONTEXT

*Leaders think and talk about the solutions. Followers think and talk about the problems.*

—BRIAN TRACY

---

**EXECUTIVE INTERVIEW 5**

**Subhashini Sharma Tripathi, Cofounder and Chief Data Scientist, Pexitics**

Authors: How would you describe the current state of artificial intelligence (AI) in your industry?

*Tripathi: We work in the HR and Analytics Industry, with products in the space of Talent Assessments and Surveys (Leadership, Core values, Competency, 360-degree feedback, Engagement Surveys, etc.). Gartner defines AI as applying advanced analysis and logic-based techniques, including machine learning, to interpret events, support and automate decisions, and take action. AI is technology that emulates human performance, typically by learning from it. Traditionally, HR has been slow to adopt technology, sometimes simply because the costing does not match the benefits for small populations of employees/small datasets. Now, with the reduction in costs of HRMS, HRIS implementations and Excel coming up with more powerful abilities to do quick and ready analytics, and technology becoming a part of MBA in HR courses, the penetration of Data Practices in the industry has increased significantly.*

Authors: In what way has AI transformed your organization?

*Tripathi: We see ourselves as an innovation cell, merging meaningful HR theories and practices with deep tech and machine learning calculations to provide meaningful insights* like *Performer Benchmarks, Laggard Benchmarks, Learning Gap Prioritization, Promotion Potential, Leadership Succession Planning, Attrition Scorecards etc. The part of AI defined as "applying advanced analysis and logic-based techniques, including machine learning, to interpret events, support and automate decisions, and take action" is our focus and we work on creating products and services around the same.*

Authors: How is AI creating value for your firm?

*Tripathi: Taking the response of Q 2 (above) forward, our revenues are wholly dependent on our products and services which have "applying advanced analysis and logic-based techniques, including machine learning, to interpret events, support and automate decisions, and take action" as a part of their intrinsic solutions.*

Authors: What do you think are current organizational challenges relating to AI?

*Tripathi: AI is still not viewed as part of a business solution. It has to be integrated with taking everyday HR decisions, and a process of continuous improvement in the AI process has to be made to make it "advanced AI—which learns from outcomes and evolves."*

Authors: What is not being done right in the AI revolution?

*Tripathi: The AI products are seen as a "ready-made" solution. However, each organization has its own culture and practices and for integration of AI, the products and services have to move from "ready-made" to "tailor-made"—which happens only when enough data has passed through the AI system. We need to give these systems the time to evolve and improve.*

Authors: Where do you think opportunities exist with regard to AI in the workplace?

*Tripathi: Within Human Resources, even though assessments and surveys have existed for long, the usage of technology and analytics to make the best decisions in the shortest possible time, use dashboards and benchmarks, etc. are yet to become the norm. These are the norm in "Customer analytics" and its success w.r.t. customers gives us hope that people management will soon see an explosion in adoption of these practices and that tools like PexiScore.com will be widely used in the future.*

Authors: In your opinion, what should and what should not be automated? Why?

*Tripathi: The most common 80 percent of the situations and decisions should be automated. These are the most standard scenarios and, if we look closely, we will find that often the decisions taken by the people management functions do not vary widely in these situations. The least common 20 percent of the situations and decisions should not be automated. It will take long to build data around these situations and decisions and, by the time data is enough, the context and culture and practices within the organization would have changed.*

Authors: How should companies prioritize AI projects? How are you doing it?

*Tripathi: As they say, follow the money. We are observing that people first adopt the basic technology of an HRMS/HRIS, then a more advanced reporting tool for dashboarding—like tableau, and finally, they realize that the information required to make good people decisions—like competency levels, latest skill levels etc., are not there. At this stage, they are likely to look for a plug-and-play model like Pexiscore.com.*

Authors: What are some of the best practices you've seen with regard to AI in the workplace?

*Tripathi: Smart companies use uniform intelligence amplification systems across the levels in the organizations—thus, the same yardstick for hiring (shortlisting and offer value generation), learning needs, compensation setting, promotions and succession planning, and tagging an attrition as desirable or not.*

Authors: Companies are part of an economic ecosystem including various stakeholders such as other companies, government, academia, and others. What role do stakeholders need to play to help AI flourish in companies?

*Tripathi: AI works on the continuous flow of data through the system. Only when each stakeholder is committed to allowing access, using the desired process and looking at the outputs, will AI flourish.*

Authors: What do you think are essential leadership attributes in the AI revolution? Why?

*Tripathi: A good leader refrains from being overenthusiastic or overcritical about AI. It may not solve all the issues today, it may be a departure from the normal today—but*

> *he appreciates the long-term impact and motivates the team to adopt AI in a phased manner.*
>
> Authors: What do you think is the future of AI in the workplace? How will work be transformed?
>
> *Tripathi: The recent coronavirus pandemic has proved that we will be dependent on digitization to survive in the future. AI will be the driver of future. Just the way aviation has adopted AI and that has helped the industry to grow so very fast, the same can be expected in the other industries. AI technologies help growth and aid good decision-making in business.*

Leaders in the age of AI need to have a keen sense of industry.

When the industrial revolution unfolded, industrialization was viewed as an opposing force to its predecessor, the agriculture revolution. Factories rose as farming became a smaller proportion in the economic equation. But at the dawn of the twenty-first century, both farming and industry are now being combined by the powerful forces of the cognitive revolution.

A drive south from Chicago gives a healthy break from the city's congestion and high-rises. Under the big blue sky, highways swirl through the cornfields. This is America's best farmland—with unmatched yields and reliable crop year after year, for centuries it has been a food supplier for the entire nation.

NatureSweet is the business of farming tomatoes. The firm realized that by using AI it can increase its yields up to 20 percent. It uses AI to study pests and combat diseases through rapid warning and intervention methods applied through AI. The firm has installed cameras that take the pictures of plants and that can rapidly identify the disease. Through continuous image analysis pest infestation or dying plants can be analyzed. This information can be used to do interventions such as targeted spraying of pesticides or other remediation steps. In addition to the imaging-based technologies, tasking technologies such as watering and seeding of crops based upon data is another part of optimized agriculture. With harvest history and data available from multiple features, the perfect timing for harvesting can also be established.

Both Democrats and Republicans have attempted to fix the immigration problem in the United States. With some of the recent steps taken by the Trump administration, illegal immigration has declined and one of the sectors feeling its impact is the agriculture sector. Historically, migrant workers played a major role in picking crops at harvest times. Now, with the labor shortage due to decline in migrant workers, California, the largest producer of fresh produce in the country, was most affected. The CEOs of large agricultural companies voiced their concerns about the labor shortage and are now proposing a creative solution: robots.

For example, Driscoll's Berries' CEO reported to *Fortune* magazine that in response to Trump-related shortage of labor, the industry is considering switching to robots. So, let us do the math—if illegal immigration is reduced on the premise that it will create more US jobs, and the employers will instead get robots, then despite reduced illegal immigration, the relevant sectors in which illegal immigrants work will not create new jobs. Of course, such a sector wide transition will create more jobs in the agri-tech sector.

In 2017, John Deere acquired a company that developed an algorithm to spot weeds. John Deere paid more than $300 million for Blue River Technology. The investment was worth it because the company can now make its weed spraying equipment that is more precise and cost-effective for farmers. John Deere is not the only company in the agriculture business that is pursuing agri-tech firms (*Financial Times*, 2018). Hundreds of agri-tech businesses are being launched to support cognitive automation of farming.

But what is new about John Deere's automated farming that we didn't see before? After all, isn't that what the company has been doing forever? The difference is that while company has been automating manual tasks, knowing what is weed and what is not, is a cognitive function. With this acquisition, we are observing the future of farmland automation as a blend of manual and cognitive functions. In fact, it is true not just for farmland, but all workplaces are being transformed where both manual and cognitive work processes are being automated.

A profession that preceded the industrial revolution and that coincided with the development of the human civilization is being transformed and improved in ways that would have seemed impossible not only for ancient Sumerians but also for farmers from the previous century.

## THE LEADER'S CHALLENGE

We provided some examples of the farming workplace being transformed by AI. The same is true for all industries. At this juncture, however, the transformation seems to be intermittent and is happening in specific functional areas or departments such as marketing, finance, human resources, and the like. This is just the beginning.

As the revolution moves forward, entire business models and value chains will experience the change.

As the AI revolution sweeps through the global economy, most executives and managers know that it has the potential to impact their businesses. With as profound a threat as major unexpected transformation in the value chain and the introduction of vastly superior business models, managers are confronted with extreme uncertainty. As competitors will crawl in from all directions, executives and managers are, or soon will be, defending their existing market share, profits, and competitive advantage.

Managers and leaders of traditional firms are not ready for such a dramatic challenge. They need guidance to understand the fundamentals of this competitive environment. In this book, we aim to guide managers on how to think about the upcoming revolution, develop insights on what is transpiring and identify ways on how to manage the changes that are taking place.

In corporate environments worldwide, traditional work processes are no longer adequate. Organizations need to gather information faster, analyze quickly, and make decisions at hyper speeds.

For companies to be competitive, they must be highly productive. For most firms, doing work is not enough. They should do work exponentially better and faster. They must do work squared.

Thus, when it comes to participating in the cognitive revolution, we need to carefully lay the groundwork in which to build key management insights.

## *Develop New Business Models with AI and Robotics*

Contemporary business models are constantly evolving. Organizations need to make adjustments in order to deal with competitive and market pressures. In the retail industry, many stores have closed due to the decline in on-site store purchases. Online shopping has dramatically reduced traditional brick-and-mortar retail sales. In response to competitive pressures and new market realities, retail stores need to find ways to lower cost and boost productivity. AI and robotics are innovative tools retailers are using to enhance operations and capture added advantages. Alarmingly, rapid changes are taking place not only in the retail industry but also in other sectors such as manufacturing and wholesale, which are also feeling pressures from emerging technologies. Business leaders need to be exceptionally adept at tracking and sensing trends and changes in consumer behavior. Business models are constantly being created, and AI and robotics have accelerated the process.

Configuring business models is no longer limited to information and mechanical automation—the cognitive part has become central.

**Business Models**

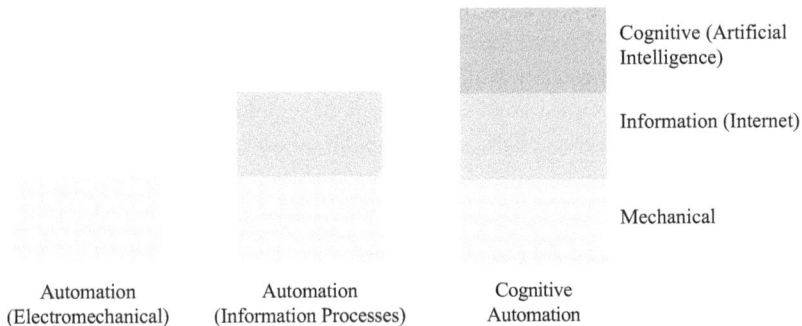

In the Cognitive automation part, it is important to recognize that intelligence, and not information or automation, is the primary source of competitive advantage. Cognitive automation will define who wins and who loses.

Think of it this way—your products or the operational equipment used to manufacture products and provide services was once solely composed of electromechanical features. In the last few decades, information was added to the basic products and equipment. For example, cars became more computerized and unlike the cars from the early 1980s when you could have opened the hood and inspected the engine with naked eye, now you run diagnostics with a computer. Your car's dashboard provides information via advanced electronics and you get all kind of data. The car of the near future, however, will have something more than just electromechanical automation and information technology—it will be autonomous. The autonomous car will have intelligence to drive better than a human and make our highways and roads safer.

## *Develop New Employee Skill Sets with and for AI*

Taking in robots and bots in the workplace presents only a partial solution. Organizations need to take on a holistic perspective and address other needs relating to the integration of robots or AI in the workplace. These needs include operational systems integration, employee training, and communication improvement, among others. The advent of AI and robotics in factories and offices worldwide has shifted the goal post. This shift requires a redefinition and realignment of the skill sets of management and employees. Careful planning is essential.

Many factories have purchased robots to boost operational productivity. It is important to bear in mind, however, that robots to do not provide a one-shot solution to all factory problems. Robots can address an important production problem. However, if not planned carefully it can lead to a Pandora's box of new problems. For example, if robots are not well coordinated with other operational functions, mishaps will happen. If employees are not properly trained or do not have the skills to manage the robots well, new problems will certainly arrive.

## *Think Differently in the AI World*

Keeping an open mind to the AI centric innovation is critical for success. For example, the publishing industry is one of the industries that has high AI integration potential. Industries that present creative opportunities to gather and analyze information can generate unique advantages. In the story, the use of an avatar for research, analysis, and insight delivery led to the creation of a potential bestselling book. The model can be replicated in several other products and industries. It is imperative that managers keep an open mind and be prepared to explore new possibilities in the AI realm. Preparedness to grow, evolve, and reinvent oneself is going to be an important attribute of contemporary and future managers.

## *AI Is Changing Both the Company's Internal and External Environments*

AI- and robotics-centric transformation does not happen in a vacuum. The AI environment impacts multiple stakeholders both internally and externally. In the case of market research companies, for instance, internal stakeholders such as the sales team, financial team, and top management are impacted by the integration of AI in their work systems. It is important to note that the external environment comprising competitors, investors, customers, government, the industry, and even society in general affects and is affected by the company's use of AI. For example, if a company's competitor aggressively uses AI, the company's sales and profitability may be impacted. In the same manner, if the company uses AI ahead of its competitors, it could gain a competitive edge and offer better value to customers and enhanced returns for investors. AI and robotics are shaped by internal and external stakeholders. In the same manner, the strong influence it yields allows it to simultaneously impact multiple parties both internally and externally. AI and robotics are part of linked operational ecosystem.

## *Develop Rapid Response to AI and Robotics Revolution*

Oftentimes, opportunities leading to organizational advantages in AI and robotics are fleeting. In many cases, being first to execute creates first-mover advantages. In some cases, a hospital that aggressively and quickly takes on new technologies can gain a distinctive edge over its competitors. More importantly, the integration of medical robotics in their work process can improve improve patient care and heighten patient satisfaction. In several organizations, a small change implemented in a timely manner can lead to a large impact. A sound AI and robotics strategy implemented too late (i.e., after all other competitors or after many customers have left) could have minimal or even adverse impact on the organization. The best AI and robotics strategy is one where the strategy is aligned with organizational competencies and market conditions, and is executed at the right time.

## *Understand the New Rules of Competition*

The basis for competition is now different. Competition is no longer just based upon information or automation—it is not driven by "intelligence." Intelligence-based competition implies that products and services that are more intelligent will generally have a competitive advantage over those that are not.

For example, in the old world, a car's performance may have been the source of competitive advantage for a firm—and for simplicity sake let us say that the only driver of competitive advantage was how quickly a car can get from 0 to 60 mph. Under this competitive environment, the firm was competing on a single variable defined by electromechanical attributes of power, that is, the functional performance. However, as the auto sector introduces autonomous cars, now another dimension is introduced into the equation. In that dimension, competitive dynamics will unfold based upon the intelligence features such as the ability of the car to understand and respond to its environment.

State 1 Leadership in AI is about utilizing technology alongside the best business context to optimize organizational performance. As Subhashini Tripathi said in the chapter interview, "follow the money."

**LEADERSHIP INSIGHT 8**: First and foremost, AI leaders need to know their business well and get their business model right.

CHAPTER 6

# STATE 2 LEADERSHIP: STRATEGIC OWNERSHIP

*A good leader thinks seriously about both the integrity of management and the management of integrity.*

—MICHAEL JOSEPHSON

### EXECUTIVE INTERVIEW 6

#### Oliver Degnan, CEO, MoreTalent

Authors: How would you describe the current state of artificial intelligence (AI) in your industry?

*Degnan: AI is widely misrepresented by technology companies and therefore widely misunderstood in terms of expectations. Tech companies often advertise their offerings in data analysis as a form of AI, disregarding the requirement for cognitive self-learning algorithmic encapsulation within the context of the business. The benefits of AI are not being realized by many new AI investments.*

Authors: In what way has AI transformed your organization?

*Degnan: Not yet. But it will in the near future. New job placements are increasingly filtered by the usage of pseudo-AI and some true AI components to mitigate the risk of wrong talent onboarding. Job placement firms and larger organizations (e.g., Marriott Hotels) are beginning to resort to AI interviews in hope of hiring top talent only.*

Authors: How is AI creating value for your firm?

*Degnan: Filtering available candidates on the open job market (e.g., Indeed.com's new AI platform) with a view to mitigating risk exponentially before interviewing the candidate. The goal is to only interview candidates that fit.*

Authors: What do you think are current organizational challenges relating to AI?

*Degnan: Leadership not pushing their respective organizations hard enough to fully embrace and understand AI benefits.*

Authors: What is not being done right in the AI revolution?

*Degnan: Tying it to the corporate bottom line.*

Authors: Where do you think opportunities exist with regard to AI in the workplace?

*Degnan: Inter-office communication. Executive communication. Workflow optimization. Determination of how well the business model (aka customer value) is being delivered daily.*

Authors: In your opinion, what should and what should not be automated? Why?

*Degnan: Hiring and firing decisions. Because of the deeply personal aspect and impact of those decisions.*

Authors: How should companies prioritize AI projects? How are you doing it?

*Degnan: Determine top-line growth and bottom-line impact in financials to justify any AI investments on the corporate (not research) levels. Examine Net Present Value over the strategic horizon to align with corporate strategy short- and long-term. Always tie AI to corporate metrics!*

Authors: What are some of the best practices you've seen with regard to AI in the workplace?

*Degnan: Educate the corporate workforce about what AI is not. AI is not a job killer! Start there, then point to working industry examples where AI is used to positively impact humans. Quickly answer the question: What does AI mean to me?*

> Authors: Companies are part of an economic ecosystem including various stakeholders such as other companies, government, academia, and others. What role do stakeholders need to play to help AI flourish in companies?
>
> *Degnan: Get out of the way!! Do not attempt to instill policies and procedures and regulations too early to not stifle AI progress too early. While at the same time, lean on established best practices and regulations.*
>
> Authors: What do you think are essential leadership attributes in the AI revolution? Why?
>
> *Degnan: Never disregard your human workforce—that is your business! AI is a competitive advantage, not a tool (e.g., AI doesn't cut through the forest; it either finds a route around it, or calls for wood-cutters with tools and cuts the forest down and sells the wood to a paper mill); either way, you lead your business to its destination faster. Leaders need to embrace algorithms as a way to make decisions. This is not the same as embracing data to make data-driven decisions.*
>
> Authors: What do you think is the future of AI in the workplace? How will work be transformed?
>
> *Degnan: AI algorithms will observe and learn the business and proactively interact with the workforce population to assist in streamlining workplace activities in the context of the business model to achieve strategic outcomes. In other words, AI will provide the workforce with a task list daily. It will not replace you via automation, but rather automate you to achieve the anticipated benefit, thus keeping you in your job longer!*

Effective leadership in the age of AI requires the uncovering of profitable business pathways, while staying ethically grounded and socially responsible.

This doesn't come easy. In fact, in many decisions being made today, executives seem to be unaware of the role AI technology can play in their firms. For example, consider the following workplace scenarios:

Human Resources: With AI companies can gain an immensely powerful insight about their employees. Using historical data from exit interviews and other human resources data, a multilateral bank in the Washington, DC, area performed analysis to determine the likelihood of employees leaving the firm. With a high confidence level, the firm could determine which employees are high-risk for leaving the firm. The analysis could further shed light upon the issues that are driving employees to leave. AI-based technology is also being applied for recruitment and staffing. In fact, with technology one can preemptively predict what openings will open up and who the most relevant and likely candidates are for hiring. Keeping the candidates engaged early on creates greater confidence in the organization and finding them quickly saves time and money. AI is also being used for interviewing candidates. From benefits analysis to creating a virtual helpdesk for employees to understand and select their benefits, AI use is in every aspect of the organization. Developing AI solutions is a complex undertaking and if competitive advantage depends upon AI, then clearly AI-related talent will be in high demand. Using AI to manage, recruit, and retain human workforce implies that the firm that will deploy AI-centered human resources solutions will be the most successful in recruitment of the AI talent. Once again, AI will guarantee its own survival.

Marketing: Engaging customers by not just understanding them but understanding them at a level where the marketer understands customers better than they understand themselves is the goal of cognitive marketing. This implies that marketers develop a deep sense of empathy and deploy tools and analysis that help them understand customers better and develop customized solutions for customers (Rossi 2017). Analysts estimate that a significant number of customer interactions are now from intelligent agents. This trend will only increase. Thus, only those companies will survive that will successfully create unanticipated shareholder value by engaging customers via AI. When viewed from a different angle, AI will ensure that it will stay with the most successful firms ( Surmacz 2017).

Finance: From managing and understanding the cost of capital to building trading platforms AI has seen its greatest use in the finance field. Now corporate finance applications are being developed that help companies allocate capital better and understand project risks in a meaningful way. Financial institutions are some of the most advanced users of AI. From achieving regulatory compliance to customer interaction management, AI drives the success of modern banking and financial institutions.

Investor Relations Management: Being able to understand and analyze shareholder expectations is fundamental to understanding how to align company's internal initiatives with the market or shareholder expectations is at the heart of investor relations management. AI technology helps with developing that critical insight. By understanding the investor sentiment and incorporating that knowledge in financial decisions, such as raising capital, firms can gain an advantage over other firms seeking capital.

Supply Chain Management: Supply Chains are being redefined with the AI technologies. Despite significant investment in supply chains, the complexity and risk of supply has increased over past several decades. With AI, firms are now developing models to implement a customer-centric cognitive supply chain. The cognitive supply chain model incorporates the point where customer becomes engaged and captures the entire value creation process in the value chain. A cognitive supply chain meets the critical requirements of rigor, responsiveness, reliability, and redundancy. It anticipates disruptions and takes preemptive actions to avoid interruptions. A firm that fails to build a cognitive supply chain will lose its advantage quickly.

More than twenty years ago, Al Naqvi experimented with neural networks for various applications including making economic forecasts, predicting futures prices, foreign exchange, and bankruptcy prediction. From his experience, the models worked in small experimental settings, but they were computationally intensive and seemed very hard to apply in production setting in business, particularly given the processing power available at that time. What is fascinating to know however, is that fairly advanced applications of AI were developed and used decades ago. It was as if the field was waiting for its time when the processing power and data will no longer be the constraints.

## EMERGING EXECUTIVE CONSIDERATIONS

Brazil was once considered a fast-growing emerging economy. In the past few years though, the country has experienced political turmoil, scandals, and economic decline. Like everything else, when an economy takes a nosedive, providing quality healthcare also becomes a challenge. In tough times, many choose to focus on immediate and ignore the future. One can observe that tendency when many healthcare systems take aggressive measures to cut down costs.

The Sírio-Libanês Hospital is located in Sao Paulo, Brazil. Considered as one of the largest hospital in South America, the hospital serves the burgeoning city of Sao Paulo, Brazil, and also gets patients from all over Brazil. One of the best kept secret of the hospital is its innovation research lab. Al Naqvi, who had the opportunity to visit the lab, was pleasantly surprised to see that several data scientists and AI engineers were busy developing solutions to help patients. This resulted from the visionary leadership of the management team and the physicians. We would like to see similar leadership in US hospitals. Despite the fact that hospitals have significant data, they tend to ignore the opportunities to develop solutions that can help patients tremendously and save lives. Hospitals tend to rely upon external product suppliers and researchers. The business challenge with AI is that solutions will not be packed in a box that can be opened, configured, and deployed. Every hospital will need to launch its own AI program. This means operating contemporary businesses strategically using a new lens:

1. Seek opportunities to be educated and build skills in AI and robotics—acquiring skills and competencies in AI and robotics puts you in a position to add value in the workplace. It also enhances your resume and expands your career prospects. Exciting careers are shaping up as a consequence of the growth in AI and robotics. Several industries are poised to benefit from AI specializations: healthcare (data-based diagnostic support), automotive (autonomous fleets for ride sharing), financial services (personalized financial planning), retail and consumer (personalized design and production), technology, communication, and entertainment (media archiving and search), manufacturing (enhanced monitoring and auto-correction), energy (smart meters), transport and logistics (autonomous trucking) (PWC 2016).
2. Be prepared to adjust to the changing AI and robotics environment—the quickly evolving nature of AI and robotics technology and architecture means that employees and organizations need to be constantly prepared to change and adapt. Speed, agility, and flexibility are important attributes for companies and employees in the coming years. Pop artist Taryn Southern created lyrics and melodies of a song titled "I am AI" but used software programs provided by AI music service providers such as Amper Music. The software program developed the instrumentals used in the song; AI developed the harmony, sequence, and cords. (McFarland 2017a). This artist adjusted to the changing AI environment and found a creative way to build a distinct competitive advantage.
3. Participate in AI and robotics initiatives—a surefire way to learn and grow in the AI and robotics field is to be involved. Participate in AI or robotics committees or research projects in your organization. Join AI and robotics professional organizations. Attend conferences and workshops in AI and robotics. The higher the level of engagement, the more meaningful the growth and development will be. Companies are partnering with universities to further their AI agenda. Boeing partnered with Carnegie Mellon University to help predict airplane maintenance schedule using autonomous intelligence technology (Rao 2017).

4. Consider operational implications of AI and robotics in the internal and external environments—AI and robotics affect stakeholders inside and outside the organization. Leaders need to carefully weigh in on what courses of action will have on diverse stakeholders. Technology and operational decisions impact multiple parties. Providing a solution for one, and neglecting another, is not exactly a positive step forward. Finding solutions in an AI and robotics environment requires taking on a broad and holistic perspective on business. Operational sustainability and social sensitivity are important considerations. A nonprofit AI research firm called Open AI, backed by Elon Musk of Tesla, aimed to promote responsible AI development (Wattles 2017a). AI farming technology, such as those developed by an Israeli digital farming company called Prospera, improves yields significantly while providing benefits both for the customers and environment (McFarland 2017b).
5. Move rapidly to capture advantages brought about by AI and robotics—speed in execution is key. Oftentimes, opportunities relating to AI and robotics are fleeting. When the right opportunity is found, employees need to be prepared to execute plans quickly. Organizational structures and processes need to be designed to accommodate speed and flexibility of action. T3, an Austin-based marketing company, quickly created a robot to capture a unique market opportunity. The firm designed a robot that analyzed Donald Trump's Twitter feed and eventually did short selling of stocks of any company that receives a negative feed from Trump. The company made money and donated the proceeds to the American Society for the Prevention of Cruelty to Animals (Wattles 2017b).

Corporations need to function and operate in innovative ways in order to manage the challenges and opportunities in an AI and robotics environment. A paradigm shift is oftentimes necessary.

## PROACTIVE MINDSET

AI leaders need to be thinking ahead and asking the right questions. Here are some key considerations:

1. Assess business operations and identify optimal operational models—an excellent way to start is to assess where the organization stands in regard to AI and robotics. Useful questions to ask include the following:

What does the company know? How does the company compare with competitors? How does it compare with the industry? What are the best practices out there? What would be excellent benchmarks? What challenges need to be addressed? Where are the solutions? How socially responsible is the business model? How can it be further improved? Knowing where the company is at with regard to AI and robotics is a good starting point.

2. Review and revitalize employee skill sets—the current employee skill sets may not be aligned with required skill sets in an AI and robotics environment. It makes sense to examine organizational operations closely to identify knowledge and skill gaps. These gaps can be sealed by providing appropriate training and developmental programs. It is important to note that employee development means a commitment toward the provision of resources. Engaging in developmental programs require a commitment of valuable resources such as time and money. When planned and executed correctly, this investment can be returned a hundredfold.

3. Engage the entire organization by forming AI circles or AI steering committees—successful implementation of AI and robotics programs requires company-wide collaboration. Programs work best when supported by top management down to the last employee. Operational breakdown can happen in any department at any level. Lackluster support even from one department can lead to program failure. In order to engage the entire organization, it might make sense to create an AI circle. This is a small group of employees and managers each representing a department. The group meets for an hour or two each week to discuss AI and robotics issues and to identify opportunities for improvement. When introducing AI and robotics for the first time in an organization, an AI steering committee can be formed to start the process.

4. Plan holistically and engage all stakeholders—planning for the successful integration of AI and robotics necessitates seeing the big picture. When implementing the program, thinking big and acting small makes sense. Meaning, one has to look at all the big pieces but provide careful attention to details in its execution. Getting internal and external stakeholders involved is an essential part of the process. Thinking through all ethical and social responsibility angles is imperative.

5. Develop a strategic AI plan and implement in phases based on priorities—creating a plan of action that ties all operational parts together is helpful.

Establishing clear goals, timelines, and priorities heightens the chance of program success. For example, while any company can develop an ambitious AI and robotics strategic plan, its actual implementation would be constrained by budgets and availability of executives. Gaining early clarity on goals and priorities would allow the allocation of resources in areas where it is most needed. The plan should be able to answer basic questions such as: What is the program and what are the priorities? Who will implement it? Why should it be implemented? When should it be implemented? Where should it be implemented? How should it be implemented? How much would it cost? How would it impact society? Considering these points would lead to more effective planning and heightens the chances for program success.

## THE AI STRATEGIC PLAN

Given the importance of a well-coordinated effort when executing an AI and robotics program, the use of an AI strategic plan is recommended.

When creating an AI strategic plan, several factors need to be considered. Listed below are key considerations and key questions to think about:

**Mission and Goals**: What are the organization's goals and objectives? What is the organization looking to achieve with the use of AI and robotics in the organization? Are the program goals aligned with the organizational goals? What should be key priorities? How does it impact society?

**Operational Assessment**: Where does the organization stand with regard to AI and robotics? How knowledgeable are the managers and employees? What do they know and what don't they know? What training and development is necessary? What operational changes need to be made?

**Market and Competitive Assessment**: What are the customer expectations in AI and robotics? How does the company stack up with regard to customer expectations? What are the best practices in the industry? What would make excellent benchmarks? How does the company compare with its competitors? What needs to get done to be competitive? What does the company need to do to deliver real value and obtain a unique competitive advantage?

**Infrastructure and Technology**: What is the status of the organization's technological architecture? What changes need to be made for the seamless integration of AI and robotics? In which areas should investments be emphasized? What should be top priorities? What are the key considerations for achieving budgets and timelines?

**Organizational Design and Preparation**: Does the current organizational structure fit the set objectives of the AI and robotics program? What changes need to be made? What areas should be emphasized? Aside from the organizational structure are there policies and processes that need to be altered? How will these changes be made and by when? What developmental programs need to be conducted for managers and employees? Are these programs aligned with established goals, budgets, and timelines?

**Relationships and Alliances**: What relationships and alliances are critical for the success of the AI and robotics program? How can internal and external relationships be strengthened? What organizational changes need to be made to optimize the value of these relationships?

**Risk Assessment**: What risk factors have to be considered in the AI and robotics program? What are the legal and regulatory considerations? How can risk be mitigated? Who should take the lead in the risk mitigation efforts? What needs to be considered in terms of cost and timelines?

**Financial Considerations**: How much does the total AI and robotics program cost? Could there be other "hidden" costs that were not initially identified? Are the financial requirements instantly needed or can it be provided in phases? Does the company have the resources at hand or will other external financial partners be required? How does the company's financial position impact established goals and timelines?

**Implementation**: What is the best pathway for the implementation of the AI and robotics program? Who should take the lead in implementing it? How should it be implemented and by when? What are the alternative courses of action if things don't happen as planned? How does the plan impact stakeholders and society?

**Review and Evaluation**: How will review and evaluation for the AI and robotics program be done? Who will conduct the review and under what timeline? How will review findings be used to improve the program? How does the program benefit stakeholders and society?

The questions listed above are by no means the only questions to be asked. The questions are shown as guides and examples. Since organizations vary, executives can refine their questions to best suit their needs.

One of Mark Munoz's business clients in the manufacturing industry posed the question during a recent factory visit: "Should a strategic plan be rigid or should it be in flux?" It was a good question and Munoz responded by saying that as technology, competition, and market forces are in flux, so should any strategic plan. The company decided to create a new management position focused on business intelligence just to promptly track rapid changes that are taking place.

Having a full-blown written plan will be helpful. A plan created by multiple members in the organization, say a planning or steering committee can contribute to program success.

The creation of the AI strategic plan is valuable in anticipating potential problems and identifying new opportunities. It can also lead to a timely and cost-efficient method in achieving program objectives. While the achievement of business goals appears to be important, of even greater importance is how these goals remain ethically grounded and become the framework for global social responsibility.

State 2 Leadership requires strategic ownership. As Oliver Degnan said in the chapter interview, "always tie AI to corporate metrics." AI leaders must be prepared to be accountable for their actions in the context of both business advancement and social responsibility. In their corporate journey, AI leaders need to be tech adventurers and stargazers equipped with a sensible moral compass.

LEADERSHIP INSIGHT 9: AI leaders need to think of their business in a holistic manner balancing profit-orientation with social passion.

CHAPTER 7

# STATE 3 LEADERSHIP: STAKEHOLDER RESPONSIBILITY

*Men make history and not the other way around. In periods where there is no leadership, society stands still. Progress occurs when courageous, skillful leaders seize the opportunity to change things for the better.*
—HARRY S. TRUMAN

---

**EXECUTIVE INTERVIEW 7**

**Arindom Basu, CEO, Digilytics**

---

Authors: How would you describe the current state of artificial intelligence (AI) in your industry?

*Basu: Digilytics operates primarily in the Financial Services industry. Very specifically, we have developed AI products for the mortgage and secured lending industry. We are finding that different participants in the mortgage industry (real estate agents, mortgage brokers, mortgage lenders, valuation surveyors and conveyancers) are at very different points of the AI curve. On the one hand, there are organizations grappling with lead time to offer of over thirty days, whereas newer digital entities are able to churn up an offer in less than twenty minutes. Lenders with advanced technology are increasingly driving the market with a significant competitive edge against traditional players with complex legacy systems.*

*The variation reflects the sizeable opportunity just in origination process for the mortgage industry. Now you can imagine the advantages of AI intervention toward the entire mortgage business value chain.*

*We find that business leaders are constantly assessing and reviewing these applications to personalize services, yield scale, and manage operative costs more efficiently, and we will see processes drastically change in the next couple of years.*

*And now, with the coronavirus crisis, AI interventions are becoming the norm rather than an exception.*

Authors: In what way has AI transformed your organization?

*Basu: We work with different mortgage industry participants in the UK and the common theme has been their eagerness to work with us to understand how best to streamline processes and adopt AI. Although each organization has a slightly different take to it, without exception, all recognize that AI is transforming their businesses to become more efficient and grow faster. As fair treatment of customers takes precedence here in the UK, lenders are trying to leverage AI-enabled journeys for customers freeing up operational time for manual intervention to handle sensitive, vulnerable cases. This bodes well for scaling loan books across the industry.*

Authors: How is AI creating value for your firm?

*Basu: Faster time to offer is the key to creating a customer-oriented differentiated product proposition. Through the AI products that Digilytics offers, we are seeing our clients transform business models with an increased focus on the brokers and customers which translate into better Net Promoter Score. More streamlined processes and less handoffs enable colleagues to do what they do best; provide more focused customer servicing.*

Authors: What do you think are current organizational challenges relating to AI?

*Basu: The organizational challenge starts with the mindset change. While business leaders aspire to transform rapidly and quite keen to drive these projects, this doesn't often permeate to every stakeholder, each with very different expectations around the benefits of such transformations, hence slowing down success. A buy-in from key business and technology stakeholders is mandatory to grant success to any AI project.*
*About deployment of AI technology, there continues to be a challenge around educating stakeholders on how AI is deployed. Lastly, AI being critically dependent on data, the challenges of gaining access to data remains a key one.*
*At Digilytics, we have developed a structured DiVA framework to rapidly deploy our AI products and realize business benefits from them.*

Authors: What is not being done right in the AI revolution?

*Basu: AI interventions are happening in silos to address discrete problems in the mortgage industry in the UK. The benefits thus are limited by to these silos. There remains a lack* of a coordinated effort across all market participants to create the data and infrastructure backbone that will allow the AI revolution to make much faster progress.

Authors: Where do you think opportunities exist with regard to AI in the workplace?

Basu: The applicability of AI is all pervasive. Any business problem, whether growth or efficiency related, has the opportunity to leverage AI to take it multiple steps forward. If there is a business problem that has been identified there is probably a smart AI solution to it.

Authors: In your opinion, what should and what should not be automated? Why?

Basu: Human relationships cannot be automated. Customer context cannot be automated. Complex decision cannot yet be automated. The collective strength of colleagues cannot be automated.
Any activity that leverages the strength of human creativity and agency should not be automated. These strengths should be augmented by automating the cognitive tasks that surround them. Anything that is data-driven, repetitive and requires basic cognitive skills should be automated.

Authors: How should companies prioritize AI projects? How are you doing it?

Basu: AI technology is here to stay and is increasingly becoming mainstream and highly accessible. Companies should look at business problems holistically and try and understand the end-state expectation. Once there is alignment on that vision, the bottlenecks that AI can eliminate are easy to navigate. Prioritization should be done on the basis of the scale of the benefits realized and the ease of implementation of these projects.

Authors: What are some of the best practices you've seen with regard to AI in the workplace?

Basu: The close alignment of business leaders and IT leaders to deliver such projects has always helped to create an achievable end-state vision. Where there is tight interaction between these functions, implementation of AI to transform businesses is faster. Additionally, access to and understanding of the data across the enterprise early in the transformation is also very beneficial.

Authors: Companies are part of an economic ecosystem including various stakeholders such as other companies, government, academia, and others. What role do stakeholders need to play to help AI flourish in companies?

*Basu: While academia and government are pioneers in creating breakthrough technologies that can aid the industry, there seems to be a disconnect around the practical applications of such technologies.*

*Academia and regulators have a great opportunity to develop AI-enabled frameworks to improve coordination between individual industry participants, such as lenders and intermediaries in mortgages.*

*Government has the opportunity to provide innovation funding to support AI programs.*

Authors: What do you think are essential leadership attributes in the AI revolution? Why?

*Basu: At Digilytics, we firmly believe that AI is here to augment human capability and create truly bionic processes and operators. Knowledge of what AI is capable of and courage to innovate business models by leveraging AI are the two largest leadership attributes in the AI revolution.*

Authors: What do you think is the future of AI in the workplace? How will work be transformed?

*Basu: Artificial Intelligence is the means forward rather than the end. As mentioned earlier, at Digilytics, we are revolutionizing business models by making the bionic with the help of AI.*

*While we see newer technologies get actively deployed in the industry and applications yet unheard of, the workforce will focus more to utilize human skills to service vulnerable customers, sensitive cases for improved financial inclusion, and fair treatment of customers. Bionic work will get more concentrated to serve specific customer requests driving an era of more personalized services.*

Faced with a multitude of challenges to keep a business enterprise thriving, leaders could get lost in the weeds. They fail to see the forest through the trees. Effective AI leaders need to be able to see the bigger picture and skillfully address the needs of multiple stakeholders.

The AI revolution, like other technological changes, is being led by few vibrant stakeholders of our economy. At the forefront are the tech giants and a handful of elite schools. Right behind them are the top-tier consulting firms and bankers. On one side is the tech media and a whole host of promoters and drumbeaters of the power of the technology. Standing right next to them are the major governments. The policy and business dynamics of the revolution are being shaped by these entities—but it shouldn't come as a surprise that a one-sided perspective is being developed.

In the middle of all this are the consumers and non-tech company executives—who are both confused and nervous about the change.

In non-tech companies, consultants are constantly knocking on the executive doors—telling everyone that if they are not on board, they will be left behind. Project success stories from one client are spun into magical tales and narrated across the industry. Old PowerPoints are out, sharpened, and redecorated with the vocabulary of intelligent automation. A consultant from a major consulting firm recently placed an ad to buy "use cases" in exchange for a world-class vacation. In other cases, consultants are selling AI projects to clients without either party understanding what the projects are for.

Vendors who have nothing to do with AI are adding AI in their menus, and universities are changing names of their digital or data programs to AI.

Media and market research firms are having a blast with report after report being released on AI.

Despite all the hype, many initial projects in AI have not been successful. The project complexity tends to be high, the tech resources are in short supply, and there is little to show in terms of success. But despite all that, billboards have appeared in major cities, and a large number of Superbowl TV commercials show AI and robots.

## RESPONSIBLE ADOPTION

The contemporary workplace as we know it, has also changed forever. The advent of AI, robotics, and related technologies is already altering the way we run business.

The changes are subtle yet deep. For instance, a company decides to purchase one robot to improve the shop-floor productivity. Seeing the benefits, management decides to purchase more and even more. The next thing you know, they have human employees doing lesser work. The productivity increase doesn't stop at mechanical automation. Slowly but surely, knowledge workers and decision-makers are also augmented and eventually replaced by smart machines. Mass layoffs begin. Managements proceed to alter their management systems and styles to incorporate the work of the robots and AI. In due time, an entirely new organization has been created. The organization has evolved.

And when evolution happens, little remains the same. Bacteria can become invincible and apes can walk on moon.

The question is not just that businesses are ready to harness the power of what lies ahead but instead whether they can control it. In our AI-related dealings with executives, we observe that they tend to be on two extremes. First, who are embracing AI technologies with open arms and can care less about any long-term impact. Second, who consider AI and robotics as antagonists and as killer robots from sci-fi movies.

When we discuss this massive change with executives, we take notice when some executives smile, shrug, and say: "I will be retired when that happens"—and we tell them: "Mr. and Ms. CEO, competitive dynamics are smiling and shrugging back at you right now. It is happening and you are in the midst of the change." The risk of denial or ignoring this powerful change is not only limited to the absence of the potential benefit that can be derived from the technology. It also includes the risk that the technology will move forward unabated and unscrutinized.

We understand that the executives may not know about what is transpiring. Very few of us do. It is still early. It is taking shape in the tech alleys and garages. But a revolution is brewing—ready to take on the world. Denial is not an option. But this is not the first time we have observed that response. Many stayed in denial when the auto sector emerged, when the Internet came, and when the information revolution took the world by surprise.

"What use could this company make of an electrical toy?," William Orton, then president of Western Union Telegraph Company, said in 1876 about the telephone. In 1946, Darryl Zanuck, executive at 20th Century Fox, said, "Television won't be able to hold on to any market it captures after the first six months. People will soon get tired of staring at a plywood box every night." In 1971, Ken Olsen, founder of Digital Equipment Corporation, said, "There is no reason anyone would want a computer in their home." And today some say, "AI belongs in fiction movies."

In a business report, the consulting firm McKinsey (2018) underscored to executives that when it comes to AI, the time to act is now. While we concur with that assessment, we would also like to add that the "acting" part must also include the governance of AI.

Consulting firms, software firms, and other profit-making entities (and that, in many cases, includes professors and universities) tend to push the adoption of technology without including an associated framework that makes the technology adoption beneficial for all stakeholders. The philosophy of responsible automation is based upon responsible adoption. Responsible adoption means ensuring that technology benefits humankind at all levels of technology's evolution—and most importantly, to do it preemptively. The key word is "adoption." This means that ethics should be considered at the time of bringing in the technology and not when the damage is already done.

Today we stand victims for decades of data thefts, data misuse, and exploitation of consumers by companies. This concern led to Senator Elizabeth Warren suggesting that the tech giants have become dangerously powerful and that they should be broken down into more competitive firms.

Lately, the rise of AI has already created instances where it has shown us signs of its abuse by humans.

We feature six stories below to showcase some of the real problems relating to AI that exists in our society today. These stories are designed to educate and intrigue. It highlights issues impacting organizations thereby requiring new pathways for AI leadership.

## A FEW STORIES

### *Spy Cab*

Laura Blanes sipped on her glass of vodka, and looked at her watch. It was 2:15 a.m.

"Why can't I ever kick this habit?" she wondered. It was the third time she was at Sandy's Bar this week.

She was with her drinking buddies earlier but all of them had left. After her recent breakup, she hated to be alone at home especially on weekends. She needed one last drink, and another, then yet another.

She felt woozy. She needed to get home.

She grabbed her mobile phone and tapped her cab app.

"Problem solved," she mumbled.

She's been using the app for six months now. All she had to do was to enter her pickup location and a privately owned car shows up and takes her home. Her GPS location shows her at the bar and she sent a request to find a driver. The AI engine on the other side received her request but it also received other data about her.

Unknown to Laura, her app was secretly spying on her. It knew that her battery was running low, the weather was bad, it was late—and most importantly she had a history of going home late from bars. In fact, using reverse logic, it was able to determine that in the past six months she used the cab app to go to

ER. Her searches while in the cab showed that she desperately sought out things to do whenever she was drunk. Her vulnerability index, politely described as "Demand Intensity Indicator," showed a score of 6 out of 10. She needed a cab soon and had limited choices.

The app buzzed and Laura received the fare estimate. It was six times the rate of the standard fare!

Laura panicked. She had very little cash on her and she had maxed out on her credit card due to her recent unexpected hospital visits.

She tried the app again, hoping it made a mistake. The app buzzed again, this time the fare estimate was seven times the standard fare! Laura cursed and slammed her phone in the bar.

An unshaven and disheveled drunk man approached her, "Everything okay?"

The man's demeanor spooked Laura. She had a bad feeling about him. His eyes were deep-set and penetrating, practically evil-looking. He smelled of dried blood masked in a mixture of alcohol and cheap cologne.

"Everything, okay?" the man yelled loudly. "Do you need a ride home? Should we go someplace else?"

Laura shook her head. "No, thank you. I have to go now." She tried to conceal her fear and hoped her quivering voice was not too evident.

Laura settled her bill quickly and ran outside. The man followed her.

She gingerly walked into the dark and slippery street and spotted an incoming taxi. She waved frantically and fortunately the driver stopped. She hopped in quickly. The drunk man trailed her by just a few feet. She shuddered at the thought of what could have happened if the taxi did not show up at that particular time.

She made it home safely and praised the heavens for her lucky break.

On her way to work two days later, she heard on the car radio that a woman who worked at Sandy's Bar went missing. She remembered seeing her at work during her last visit. Could that drunk man who chased her out of the bar have something to do with her disappearance?

It was a disconcerting thought. She vowed to stay out of the bar scene. She cursed the AI-powered cab app and how it pushed her into danger.

## *Travel Planner*

It was 10:00 p.m. in the evening and John Cruz was busy working in his home office in Miami, Florida.

He stopped abruptly. He just remembered he needed to book a flight and hotel in order to visit his sick mother in New York. He makes it a point to visit her every month, sometimes every two weeks to attend to her needs. Her cancer has spread and he feared her life is nearing the end. He wished his job was not that far away.

He proceeded to make the travel arrangement through his favorite travel website. He noticed that the price seems to be increasing all the time, especially in instances when he books the trip close to the departure date.

Unknown to John was the fact that his favorite website is a mega-learner. The AI-driven system knows and had learned almost everything about him—his schedule, preferred destinations, prior trips, car rental details, and even the food he eats whenever he travels. It knew he frequently visited one cancer care hospital and knew he's been paying bills for an elderly woman in New York. It knows that the regular trips to New York are very important to John. It knows that given the importance of the New York trip, John will pay whatever amount is necessary.

The travel quote appeared and John was astounded. It was triple the price of the usual fare from Miami to New York. He knows this for a fact because one of his clients just took a similar trip on business and paid roughly a third of his quoted price.

John tried booking through another website. Again, the travel quote was identical.

John is unaware that information is shared across different AI architecture, and companies share information. The travel companies know exactly what John wants when he travels and that he desperately needs to travel to New York. The website even offered services that John might be interested in such as flowers upon arrival in New York, cancer care specialists in the New York area, private nurses and care givers and even funeral services.

Having no other options, John booked the trip to New York.

When he got to his mom's hospital room, he immediately gave her a hug and kissed her. Mary, his mom, looked so pale and weak.

"How are you, mom?" he asked.

"I'm fine, son. Just trying to get better," Mary said weakly.

"They're treating you okay, here? Is there anything you'd like me to get you?"

Mary was quiet and deep in thought. "I'd like us to discuss funeral arrangements."

John was uneasy. "Mom, we shouldn't talk about these things yet. You will get better soon."

"I think we have to. I've been seeing a lot of ads about funeral services. I think it's a sign," Mary said.

"What are you talking about?" John asked.

He took her iPad and looked at the screen. Right beside the news network were five ads about funeral services. The news network knew she was sick and tailored several ads to prepare her for her possible death.

John was fuming mad. How could they do this to his mom? Rather than encouraging her to fight for life, the AI-driven machine recommended preparing for death. How insensitive?

John shook his head. "Mom, it's not a sign. I get these types of ads too. You should be thinking about recovery, not this kind of thought."

Mary coughed heavily for several minutes, panting for breath. She was exhausted and went to sleep.

John stared sadly at his mom. Indeed, her days were numbered. He remembered the times they spent together, his childhood, and the ways the world changed over time. He pondered on how the advent of technology made things great and horrible at the same time. He wondered about AI and how it can practically bring people to the edge. It can hurt the vulnerable. It can even lead them to their deaths.

He remembered his travel website. He recalled seeing several funeral services ads. He didn't make the connection until now. The AI-driven website knew everything about him and his mom. His virtual "travel agent" had planned not only for his trip but for his mom's last trip as well.

## *Virtual Recruiter*

Mike Jones, vice president for Human Resources, was listening to the phone's earpiece, cringing. The CEO of the company, Anne Smith, was yelling at him from the other end of the line.

Anne said, "What do you mean you haven't made the hire yet? It's been two months! I asked you to use every tool in your disposal to hire the right candidate. We need that Global Market Research Analyst asap!"

Mike rubbed his forehead, frustrated, "Anne there are protocols we need to follow. We need to consider legalities. It's a high-profile role, the HR community, the media, and our stakeholders are watching. We can't rush this and fumble."

Anne was angry, "Enough of these lame excuses! If we don't get that position filled in the next two weeks, we may not have a company to run next year. Fix this problem, Mike. Fix in now!"

She slammed the phone.

Mike stared at the phone for a few seconds and placed it down gently. His boss was a character alright. At times he hated her guts, but often admits to her being passionate and driven to succeed. Anne made their luxury retail company highly successful despite a trying environment. They badly needed to hire a Global Market Research Analyst to support their global expansion efforts. While domestic sales were dwindling, overseas sales were skyrocketing. They badly needed an expert with strong market research skills to understand global consumers and help identify the best expansion locations.

He was hesitant about using a subscription-service employment search engine. The sales rep visited him a couple of times in the past two months. He pitched their service as a "virtual recruiter" who scouted the web, social media, and international databases to find the right candidate. The service offering was far cheaper than the typical employment recruitment service.

Mike liked the idea, but was concerned about his company's widely advertised policy about inclusion and diversity. How can the "virtual recruiter" be really fair in qualifying candidates? How can there be certainty that the process was fair? Might the system be rigged?

Facing the pressure from Anne, he decided to give the company's sales rep a call.

"Gene Gilbertson, good morning." It was a deep, cheerful voice from the other line.

"Gene, this is Mike Jones. How are you?"

"Great, good to hear from you, Mike. How can I help you today?"

"I'm thinking of giving your system a try," Mike said with some skepticism in his voice.

"Well, I actually have something ready for you. You already gave me a job description, salary range, desirable qualifications and skills, corporate culture, desired personality, attributes and values, and coworkers' profile. I already created a file for you. Once you say go, I will press the start button and a list of candidates will emerge that closely matches your desired profile."

"Great! Send me the list of candidates when it's ready," Mike said, still skeptical.

"I actually just pressed Enter. I have the list right now in front of me. Do you have Skype? We can go through the list together now."

Mike was impressed. "Man, you're fast."

They connected via Skype and looked at the top 10 list together.

"Very impressive list." Mike was impressed. "These are all excellent candidates."

"The power of artificial intelligence," Gene said proudly. "As mentioned, our service is top rate, superfast, and very inexpensive compared to the other options. It's also global in reach.

Mike paused, "Hold on, these are all White males, all living in metropolitan locations. Can you run the top 20 please?"

"Sure!" Gene said.

The results were the same—White males residing in metropolitan areas. Great candidates but all with the same profile. There was not a single female or minority in the list.

Mike was starting to be uncomfortable. "Let's run the top 50."

Same results.

"Do the top 100 now," Mike said, disturbed.

Same results.

"How can you explain this, Gene?" Mike asked. "There's not a single female or colored person in the list."

Gene was stumped, too. "Hmm ... I used all the parameters you mentioned and applied that algorithm."

Mike shook his head. "This is not going to work, Gene. If someone gets hold of the fact that we used this process, my company will get into trouble."

Gene nodded. "I see where you're coming from. Think of this as a tool to supplement your current search efforts. It would be one of the many tools you are currently using. We found a few good candidates, didn't we?"

Mike rubbed his forehead, again frustrated. "We did, but it doesn't seem like a fair process. It excluded so many other great candidates out there. How many clients did you say you have?"

"Thousands," Gene said proudly.

Mike was very disappointed. "Sorry, Gene. This doesn't work for me. I'd much rather recruit people in a fair, old-fashioned way."

He stared at the phone and reminisced his long corporate career. He rose through the ranks. Hired thousands of people, many of them from diverse backgrounds. He made excellent hires, and changed many lives.

He knew exactly what to do. He'll call Anne and stand his ground. It's his way or into the highway.

## *The Infiltrators*

The General sat still in the driver's seat of his car. He carefully surveyed the surroundings of the isolated villa. It was pitch black. The only faint light came from the library of the house. It was an indication that the President was awake.

No one was in sight.

The President sent everyone away for the night, including all his security staff.

This was a highly clandestine and personal meeting between the President and the General.

The General quietly stepped out of the car. He looked over the surroundings one more time and walked toward the villa. He rented the villa under the name of a friend a week ago. He had the place carefully inspected to make sure there were no listening devices. Except for his two security aides, no one else knew the President was in the villa. The General organized such matters well and with the highest attention to detail. His thoroughness led to his rapid rise in rank.

The General tapped the door twice.

The President opened the door. He was impeccably dressed and looked youthful. He exhibited a calm yet ruthless demeanor.

"Come in, General," the President said coldly.

"Good evening, Mr. President," the General said politely, shaking the President's hand. "I suppose you have everything you need in the villa."

"Yes, General. Thank you. As usual, you have planned well. I actually like this place. Love the view of the mountains. We should use this place more often," the President said smiling.

"We could only use each meeting place once, Mr. President."

"I know, I know," the President said. "Come let's sit in the library. I have a bottle of scotch ready."

The President poured a generous amount of scotch in two glasses, and handed one glass to the General.

He took a sip from his glass, and stared at the General intently. "Tell me General, how are we progressing in our target country." He was referring to a country that both men vowed to destroy a year prior. They hated the country's politics. Furthermore, the country's economy was a major threat to theirs. There was a personal matter too. Both of them lost a loved one from a previous conflict with the target the country. The President lost a brother in the war, the General lost a son. To both men, destruction of the target country meant a total revenge.

The General smiled uncharacteristically. In fact, the President wondered if this was the first time he ever saw the General smile.

"We have made very good progress, Mr. President," the General said, putting down his glass on the coffee table. "As you know, I've assembled a highly talented and discreet team of AI experts to fuel both political camps with inflammatory ideas. It worked really well. The media bots exploited human vulnerabilities and increased social conflict. Both camps are at each other's throats and they are now at the brink of a civil war."

The President was pleased. "Excellent. How's their economy doing?"

"It's a mixed bag," the General said confidently. "Some sectors in the society benefited from the chaos. Companies that created marketing bots made money from all the political drama and turmoil. The media benefited from the news exposure. Many publishers capitalized on the political garbage and sold a lot of books."

The President interrupted him. "Yes, I've seen some of the news accounts. The events have been broadcasted globally."

"It's been circulated in all forms of media. Horrible publicity. The country now appears to be a war zone with chaos on the streets. One sector that's gaining from this mess is the defense and arms industry. Arms manufacturers sold a lot of weapons due to the rising armed conflict."

"So, it has been somewhat good for their economy," the President wondered.

"In some sectors, yes, but mostly it had a negative effect. Their currency has recently devalued. Foreign investors have shied away from investing in the country. Trade of goods has declined and prices of commodity have gone up. They now have double-digit inflation. A total financial crisis is just around the corner."

The President smiled. "The country is in shambles, then. Yes?"

The General smiled back. "Make that a big YES. A very big YES."

Both men laughed.

The General thought of his AI team back in the headquarters. What a wonderful team, he thought. He marveled at the power of AI and its ability to infiltrate and destroy a country.

The General looked at the President intently, and said, "What country should we go for next?"

## *Better Than Cocaine*

Dr. Jake Blacksmith looks at a glass panel showing his "lab". It doesn't look like a lab at all. It looks more like a day-care center. Offering high incentive fees to parents, his team of scientists and tech experts develops algorithms to get children more engaged in social media. His "lab" had a dozen young children ages 3–12 tinkering with an assortment of tech devices. The scientists who were supervising the experiment looked and were dressed like day-care attendants.

He smiled at the thought of how laboratories have evolved in recent years. Actually, he just realized, the whole world is his laboratory. His team can capture and analyze data on web and mobile phone usage of people from all over the world. As long as consumers visit the company's various educational and recreational websites and apps, all information is fair game. Every user is a virtual lab subject. Following this logic, it dawned upon him that he had millions of subjects worldwide.

He felt strong and powerful. His company was in a unique position to understand the world and even shape the way it thinks and acts. He captured his potential consumers early. He controlled their minds starting at childhood. It was a time when they were most vulnerable and his influence is strongest. As CEO, he was the world's chief influencer.

On this particular day, two members of his company's Board of Directors were with him. They too were staring at the children through the glass panel.

Melanie Brown, a cofounder and best-selling psychology author, appeared disturbed. "Jake," she said. "You saw the latest tech analysis, right?"

Jake nodded. "Of course, I did."

Melanie looked at him. "Well, does that not bother you?"

Jake shrugged her off. "Why should it? It shows our design and developed algorithm is effective. We have successfully influenced the thinking of children worldwide. We have had consistent success over the years. We know exactly what they want and how to tweak their preferences."

Gil Gomez, the company's Technology Advisor jumped in. "I agree, we get the students engaged. We educate them in new ways and accelerate their learning."

Melanie glared at both of them. "Are you saying that manipulating of minds and brainwashing is learning? Wake up guys, what we're doing is borderline unethical and illegal. We get these students addicted to the games and devices. The latest tech analysis shows that these children's games are more addictive than cocaine!"

Jake looked at her. "Look, Melanie. I see what you're saying. But, we've built a successful and highly profitable company over the years. We're a globally recognized and loved brand. We shape global thinking."

Melanie moved away from the glass panel. "Exactly," she said. "That's precisely why we need to reconfigure our system to do what's right. We have to steer the world toward the right direction."

Jake was curious. "And to what direction are you referring to?"

Melanie stepped closer. "Jake, we started this together. We wanted to help sick kids and the physically challenged. We have commercialized our model beyond belief. This is no longer the vision we first developed. This algorithm has turned into a monster. It's playing with the minds of the kids. It's controlling them."

"We are not controlling them!" Gil interrupted abruptly.

"You're right," Melanie said. "We are not controlling, the machine is. We are instigators and facilitators of the process. We too are being used by the machine. It knows we want profit and influence and feeds into our desires. If there's something we accomplished, we've created the ultimate mind manipulating machine."

Jake saw her point. "So, what do you want us to do?"

"Destroy the machine," Melanie said firmly.

Jake was shocked. "Are you out of your mind? We spent hundreds of millions building this! We did this to improve lives!"

"Well, did we?" Melanie asked sarcastically. "You have three kids, Jake. Gil, you have two. I have a daughter and she has been using the product. She is addicted, guys. I know your kids are too. Our company is messing with the minds of a future generation. A machine is controlling the whole process. Heck, we can't even technically control this machine. It follows its own path and runs its own course!"

Gil looked down dejectedly. "My kids are actually addicted too. They hardly talk to me. The machine has become their parent, teacher, and friend."

Jake looked bothered. "My kids are addicted, too. They've exhibited strange behavior. I have started taking them to a psychiatrist. You're right, Melanie. It's doing something strange."

Suddenly, they heard yelling from the lab. The kids were yelling at each other. Two kids started pulling each other's hair. The scientists were trying to control the situation.

Melanie looked at Jake. "Jake, please do the right thing. This has got to stop."

Jake pondered on the magnitude of the situation. It would take a vast amount of time, effort, and resources to undo this mess. He would need to be totally humble and honest. He would need the support of the government, media, educational institutions, and the business community worldwide. He had to do it and had to do it now.

He said quietly, "I will, Melanie. I will."

## *The Art of Winning*

Michael Shapiro and Doug Leblanc were enjoying dinner at an ultra-high-end restaurant in New York. The two men shared an apartment when they were at law school 20 years ago. They have decided to meet and catch up. They have not seen each other in 10 years.

"Cheers to you, Doug," Michael said, raising his glass.

"Cheers to you, Michael," Doug said.

"Thanks, Doug. Who would have thought we'd make it this far?" Michael asked. "Law school was a real struggle for both of us."

Both men laughed. They remembered how happy they were just to get a passing grade.

"Fate's been kind, my friend," Doug stated, as he repositioned his table napkin. "Most specially to you my friend. Heck, did you even ever lose a case? I read about you from time to time in the newspaper. You never lost a case, did you?"

Michael sipped on his water, then humbly said, "I lost a few early in my career. Just got better over time. These new technologies have been helpful."

"Which technologies?" Doug asked curiously.

"I'll tell you a little secret my friend. Not be shared with anyone, okay?" Michael stated.

"Promise. Hell you know me. Did I ever share with anyone the crazy antics you did at law school? You know I could keep secrets," Doug said, looking somewhat offended.

"I know. No offense, my friend. You're like a brother to me. But, this is very sensitive information. I just want to make sure you understand this should never be spoken about outside of this table."

"Got it. Tell me," Doug said with heightened curiosity.

"My law firm has invested heavily in AI. We've invested tens of millions. As a result, our firm has algorithms that analyze cases based on win-ability, the media coverage the case would get, the personalities of the judges and opposing attorneys, best strategies to influence the judgment of the judge and even the jury. It provides an analysis of the words our attorneys will need to use to resonate more with a certain type of jury member."

Doug was astonished. "Holy S——! What the f...?"

Michael continued, "Also, the ability of the client to pay fees."

Doug couldn't hide his amazement. "Jesus ... Isn't that illegal?"

Michael looked surprised. "You know we're talking about a law firm right? We know the law like the palm of our hand. We know what can be done, and what can't."

Doug shook his head. "I probably meant unethical, rather than illegal."

Michael nodded. "Ethics is an entirely different issue."

Doug sipped on his glass of wine. "If that's the case, I would never ever want to be against you in a courtroom. I wouldn't stand a chance."

Michael smiled. "It wouldn't only be you, Doug. All other attorneys, all other law firms would have a slim chance of winning. We haven't lost a single case since we set up our AI department."

"Amazing stuff!" Doug exclaimed. "If I didn't know you well enough. I would have thought this was all science fiction."

"It isn't just us, though. Many other law firms are exploring the space. We know. They've started offering seven-figure salaries to try to recruit some of our AI team members. It's the new legal ballgame, Doug. This isn't the future, it's a current reality."

Doug was pensive. "Wouldn't this skew the justice system?"

"The justice system is already biased toward the rich and influential. What difference does this make?"

"It will distort it even more and accelerate the process. Scale it up in a grand way. Twisted legal system squared. Slanted law—global."

"You no longer seem impressed," Michael said, teasing his friend.

"No, I'm very impressed, but also very disturbed," Doug mumbled.

"A secret, right?" Michael said.

"A secret," Doug promised. He sipped on his glass of water.

From his table, Doug stared out of the window. It was a chilly night in Manhattan. Suddenly, he felt gloomy. He stared at the multitude of people walking on the crowded streets several floors below. He wondered if any of them would have a chance for justice under this new AI-influenced legal architecture.

## BEYOND THE STORIES

These were not just mere stories. While fictional, they are based upon events that are currently happening all around us. They underscore the potential and the perils of adopting AI. Clearly, if we are encountering all this when we have barely touched the tip of the iceberg, the prognosis for the future does not look good.

What that means is that in the course of all the excitement associated with AI, we must proceed with caution. We must accept responsibility for the welfare and safety of our companies, its stakeholders, and society in general.

Adoption of new technology is good, but it should be accompanied with responsibility. Leaders should be able to think broadly and to think in new ways.

State 3 Leadership in AI is about embracing stakeholder responsibility. As Arindom Basu mentioned in the chapter interview, *"a buy-in from key business and technology stakeholders is mandatory to grant success to any AI project."* This underscores the need to know oneself, what one truly believes in and how one relates with others. AI leadership requires a keen understanding of personal and organizational strengths and weaknesses. It underscores the need to truly understand the soul of the corporation and its relationship with humanity.

> **LEADERSHIP INSIGHT 10:** In the era of AI, leaders need to be both cognitive and mindful. They need to master their own souls and the souls of their organizations. AI leaders need to have a high sense of connectivity with themselves and society.

CHAPTER 8

# AI LEADERSHIP AND THE WAY FORWARD

*A true leader has the confidence to stand alone, the courage to make tough decisions, and the compassion to listen to the needs of others. He does not set out to be a leader, but becomes one by the equality of his actions and the integrity of his intent.*

—Douglas MacArthur

---

**EXECUTIVE INTERVIEW 8**

**Sanjoe Jose, CEO, Talview**

Authors: How would you describe the current state of artificial intelligence (AI) in your industry?

*Jose: AI is still at infancy in the HR world. We have made some progress in the last two years, with HR and recruitment professionals adopting AI tools such as chatbots, AI-based video interviews, proctoring bots, and resume-matching tools. However, we expect AI to become a bigger priority as many CEOs are mandating investments in AI-based tools across verticals to solve critical business challenges. In line with this trend, in the recent past we have seen a lot of businesses investing in AI-powered HR tools to solve the key challenges, and these challenges show a direct impact on the revenue of an organization. The fear of losing jobs to AI is still present amongst a few business executives; at the same time, a lot of Gen X and Gen Z workforce have seen the value in AI as augmenting their capability than replacing them, and soon we can expect to see massive adoption of AI in HR.*

---

Authors: In what way has AI transformed your organization?

*Jose:* When I founded my last startup InterviewMaster in 2013, which was an asynchronous video interview solution for distributed hiring, we didn't have AI as an ally. However, when we launched Talview in 2017, we were AI-enabled from day 1. Looking back while both delivered value for our customers, the ROI for customers in Talview is multiples of what InterviewMaster could do because it is not just a tool which helped them to digitize a process but also drive intelligence and insights for much higher efficiency. That helped us to differentiate ourselves from our competitors and partner with some of the largest companies in the United States.

Authors: How is AI creating value for your firm?

*Jose:* Talview's vision is to build the fastest way to hire for enterprises and we wouldn't be able to do it without AI powering a significant part of the value proposition. We've leveraged AI and ML to automate and drive more insights—all the way from the top of the hiring funnel right through to the moment of hire. From the start of the process, these technologies are used to screen resumes, derive additional insights from interviews and expertly match candidates to their ideal roles. As the candidate goes through each step from the location of their choice, computer vision is leveraged to authenticate their identity and administer multiple variety of skill-based assessments. During the interview process, the technology assists hiring managers in conducting an objective interview—by building a behavioral profile of the candidate that leverages speech recognition and natural language processing, and giving suggestions as to areas hiring managers should probe from a non-technical skills standpoint. With companies struggling to assess soft skills accurately, these kinds of behavioral reports help companies hone in on communication, interpersonal, and leadership skills.

Authors: What do you think are current organizational challenges relating to AI?

*Jose:* The biggest challenge is inability of organizations to understand AI. Many confuse AI as just data science and assume if they do not have quality data internally they cannot leverage AI. This is often a result of vendors who camouflage regular analytics service as AI failing to deliver any tangible value to the customer. It is not a must that you need data internally and you can engage vendors who have built meta-intelligence by working with multiple customers in the industry. Another challenge in adoption. There is a fear about AI; often working professionals think that AI will take their job away. The fact is it's helping businesses to solve critical challenges with faster turnaround time, and it's helping employees to be more productive and add more value. AI is creating new markets and new jobs in the industry.

Authors: What is not being done right in the AI revolution?

*Jose:* We often hear AI is biased. However, if built correctly AI is the way to eliminate human bias. To start with, the AI engineers and Data Scientists need to ensure that training data is diverse and includes different groups. Once developed it has to be continuously monitored to identify, isolate, and eliminate attributes which are causing any form of bias. However, very few organizations are doing it right.

Authors: Where do you think opportunities exist with regard to AI in the workplace?

*Jose:* There are a lot of areas AI can be leveraged in the workplace; my five top areas are

- *AI for productivity and work-life balance*
- *To remove human bias and increase diversity*
- *Employee experience*
- *Upskilling employees and minimizing the skill gap*
- *AI for sourcing and screening new Talent*

Authors: In your opinion, what should and what should not be automated? Why?

*Jose:* The tasks which are high volume, mundane, and repetitive, those that don't require human intervention should be the first to be automated. If there is a task which has been done in the same way for a long period of time, without many variables, it doesn't have to be done by a human. The tasks that vary highly, require empathy and emotion should not be automated. AI doesn't have empathy and can't engage humans as other humans do.

Authors: How should companies prioritize AI projects? How are you doing it?

*Jose:* One will always find a lot of potential areas to implement AI. Our priority framework for AI projects is not different from the one we use for other projects—maximum impact with minimum efforts. And project identification and prioritization has to happen independent of AI. AI should be brought in if that is the best solution for the most important projects. Customer feedback is also critical to shaping your AI project; involving a few key customers for validating the AI projects helps a lot. We continuously hear from customers, their challenges and see how we can solve their challenges by using any technology and need not always be AI. During solutioning, if we realize that AI is the best solution for a priority problem then we pursue that direction. During the entire process, our team works with industry experts and Talview's customer advisory board.

Authors: What are some of the best practices you've seen with regard to AI in the workplace?

*Some of the best practices for AI in the workplace are:*

1. *Use AI only where it is required; do not force fit*
2. *Focus on outcome delivered and not the complexity of the solution*
3. *Institutionalize process to continuously monitor outcome for fairness/bias*
4. *Celebrate successes, discuss failures, learn from them, and move forward*
5. *AI is still at its infancy as a technology, lot of experts can be imposters and hence build your team carefully*

Authors: Companies are part of an economic ecosystem including various stakeholders such as other companies, government, academia, and others. What role do stakeholders need to play to help AI flourish in companies?

*Jose: The biggest role for the ecosystem to play is to ensure fair application of AI. From providing guidelines to ensure fair use to democratization of data should be driven collectively by the ecosystem keeping objectives of all the groups in view. Collaboration and shared learning can fast track evolution of this nascent field at a faster pace benefiting everyone.*

Authors: What do you think are essential leadership attributes in the AI revolution? Why?

*Jose: In the age of AI, leaders can bring revolutionary changes in the economy or in the workforce by deciding to invest in the right areas. Some of essential attributes in my opinion are as follows:*

1. *Vision plays a significant role in effective leadership, a great visionary leader can bring digital transformation while keeping the focus on long-term goals.*
2. *Humility. Leaders should open to hear feedback from the organization on what is working and what needs to be improved.*
3. *Adaptability is another leadership attribute that will drive the AI revolution. Not being afraid to take new courses of action in the technology when there is a new opportunity or business threat can help businesses or governments to bring digital transformation.*
4. *Driving Engagement top-down during the AI journey builds trust and faith. This can help organizations and workforce to follow the vision while going through the transformation.*

> Authors: What do you think is the future of AI in the workplace? How will work be transformed?
>
> *Jose: AI is not going to replace humans but augment human capabilities to be superhumans. Every aspect of work is continuously reinvented and AI is going to be a primary driver in this reinvention in the coming years. The core themes which are emerging are as follows:*
>
> 1. *Every employee will have digital assistants to help with the mundane tasks, this will also increase employee productivity and satisfaction.*
> 2. *Real-time insights and predictive analytics for better and quick business decisions.*
> 3. *Job descriptions will evolve in line with the above changes with more focus on human ability for empathy, relationship building, and dealing with unknown.*

In the past chapters, ten leadership insights were offered as key considerations for executives looking to effectively manage enterprises in an emerging cognitive society.

It is evident from these insights that significant changes are taking place in the workplace. It has taken the practice of management and leadership into an entirely new frontier.

In this concluding chapter, we provide additional context to those leadership insights and dig deeper into what the implications are in the contemporary workplace. Furthermore, we explore what all these might mean as we move into the future.

To invoke your imagination, we've created workplace scenarios to help you think through day-to-day interactions with AI and what this might mean to regular employees and organizational leaders.

These scenarios have been intentionally exaggerated in the context of the current state of technology. The purpose of the scenarios is to demonstrate that leadership decisions today sets the foundation of what happens tomorrow. As you read these scenarios, think about your own workplace and the changes AI will potentially bring about in the coming years.

## WORKPLACE SCENARIOS

### *Louella, Retail Store Cashier*

Louella walked hurriedly into the store. She stole a glance at her watch. "Damn, late again," she thought.

"You're late," a stern female voice from the cashier's desk boomed. It was from Jean, the shift supervisor.

Louella looked apologetic. "So sorry. I had to drop Joe at the day care and the owner didn't open up on time. I had to wait for about 30 minutes."

Jean glared at Louella. "You can't keep doing this. You know lots of talented college girls would be very happy to take a job like yours."

"I know, it won't happen again," Louella said dejectedly. "I'll find a more reliable day care that opens much earlier."

She started her usual morning routine—arranging the desk, organizing the clothes rack and displays, and cleaning the retail space. As she was doing the chores, she couldn't help thinking about the future. How fragile was her financial position? It was tough being a single mom, especially when you have a sickly son. Earning a bare minimum wage was not helpful, but it's the only job she can find. She wanted to find a second job, but Joe's poor health needed much attention. She's been living from paycheck to paycheck. How bleak her future looked like?

She moved toward the front end of the store. No customers yet. It's still early. She hoped many will show up today. She needed the sales commissions badly. Online sales have impacted her sales dramatically. The decline in the number of people visiting the mall was noticeable. What was it, a 20 percent decline? Maybe, even more. People now prefer to buy goods online. It's much more convenient. Heck, even she's been buying online. With her tight schedule, it's the only way to go.

Her cell phone buzzed. It was her friend Kate. "How are you?" the text message read.

She glanced at Jean, she's busy looking through financial records. Quickly Louella typed back, "All good."

Another buzz came from Kate. "Sorry, I couldn't help you out with Joe today. Couldn't leave work."

"No worries. Let's get together during the weekend and discuss our new plans." Louella's friend Kate was in a similar boat. Kate works as a nurse aide and has been spending most of her earnings caring for her sick mother. They have been friends for years. They were classmates in a computer programming class years ago. They both actually did very well in that class. They aced most exams. It's a pity they both didn't get to complete their college degree. A degree or even a certificate in Information Systems could help them land good paying jobs. Kate mentioned a crash course on artificial intelligence. It was a three-week certificate program. They both thought it might help open up new career paths for them. They agreed to meet again to concretize their plans.

Two men carrying large boxes entered the store.

One of them mumbled, "Hi, is Jean Brown in?"

Louella nodded. "She's over there."

Jean waved to the men. "Over here!"

The men spent the entire morning assembling a robot. Louella overheard that the robot can follow customers, greet them, answer any questions they have, and have buttons ready to allow customers to pay and check out. The robot can even pick out non-paying customers and can alert mall security in seconds.

In a few hours, the men had assembled a five-foot-tall robot. It looked alike much like R2D2 of *Star Wars*, but instead of legs it had wheels at the bottom for quick mobility across the retail floor. The robot's chest had a touch-screen panel that enables customers to scan their credit cards and pay for their purchases. The robot can interact fully and can answer customer questions instantly.

One of the men said excitedly, "This here could boost your sales productivity by 70 percent easily. It would also lower your operational cost in the long run. Plus, it would excite your customers. It would arouse their curiosity. I'm telling you. Your sales will increase. We've seen it happen in other stores."

Jean had a sullen look on her face. "No need to sell to me. This was already approved by headquarters. I'm just here to implement this plan. Can anyone tell me how to manage this robot?"

The second man spoke, "It's so easy. We'll train you. There's a manual, but it's all easy. Push of the button."

Jean was not convinced. "Do I have to charge him every day?"

The second man shook his head. "Nope, he walks to his station and charges himself."

Jean was astonished. "You mean, he'll do all the sales work, cashiering, and even power himself up?"

The second man nodded. "Yes, and he creates all the reports for you and sends it to headquarters."

Jean's eyes were wide open. "Wow! I guess I'll have to learn how to manage a robot."

The first man interjected, "No need, we've got that taken care of too. All push button, self-managed."

Jean looked over the invoice and signed. "Uh-oh… it looks like I may be out of a job soon."

The two men laughed.

Louella smiled nervously. "I may be out of a job soon," she thought. "The robot practically could do all of my job and more. And, he'll never be late."

In the next two weeks, the robot called Ro-A did all tasks with amazing speed and efficiency. The customers loved him. His stored memory of jokes and cool quips never ceased to impress the customer. He can even sense the customer mood and adapts the conversation style based on how the customer feels. He recites all the prices and discounts automatically and quickly arranges out-of-stock orders. Sales have gone up dramatically.

The introduction of Ro-A in the workplace changed their business model. It was no longer business as usual, in fact it was more like business unusual.

One morning, Jean called Louella to her office.

Jean looked at her sadly. "I'm sorry, but I'm giving you a two-week notice of employment termination. You'll be entitled to all the benefits outlined in our contract."

Ro-A entered the room with a stack of merchandise. "Hello ladies," he said, "Mind if I leave these items here? Have a good day!" He rolled out of the room cheerfully.

Louella couldn't help her amusement.

She saw this day coming. "Did a robot replace me?"

Jean nodded sadly. "In a way, he did. Soon, he may replace me too."

Louella wiped a tear in her eye. "How can I possibly compete with something like that?"

Jean gave a consoling look. "We can't, we'll need to find our own special skills fast to compete in the workplace. Soon we'll have Ro-A's in all retail stores across the country."

Louella stood up. "Okay, I'll get back to work now. I'll think of something."

Jean stammered, "I'm so sorry, Louella. If ever you need a reference, I'm here for you."

Louella quietly mumbled, "Thanks."

She walked toward the retail floor.

## *Ben, Factory Worker*

Ben arrived a little late for lunch at the factory cafeteria.

His buddies Rick and Jim were seated in the usual spot and were halfway done with their meal.

Ben quickly gathered some lunch items and walked toward his buddies. "May I join you?" he said.

Rick, a robust, bearded 55-year-old, smiled. "Certainly. We saved a seat for you."

Jim, a thin man with thick eye glasses, pointed at the vacant seat. "Late today, huh?"

Ben placed down his tray and started to eat. "Yes, I had a long meeting with Larry, my shift supervisor." He paused and gulped down his drink. "We've had too many breakages in our unit."

Rick looked surprised. "How so? Didn't you have a new robot to assist you?"

Ben nodded while quickly swallowing his food. "Yes, did you see that 8 foot tall RoboCop-looking contraption?"

Jim butted in, "Who could possibly miss that? Isn't that supposed to make your work easier?"

Ben nodded. "Sure, but we're going through an adjustment stage. The guys working with the robot is still learning the coordination process. Meanwhile, many mishaps happened. One guy pressed the wrong button and the robot ended up breaking 50 units. Another guy accidentally hit the robot with a pole and toppled it. One day, I keyed in the wrong programming code and it stopped working for several hours. There's many more. What a mess!"

Rick sipped his water and added, "Well, factory personnel need to be trained on robot management. You can't just put robots in the factory floor and expect everyone to seamlessly adapt."

Ben looked at him pensively. "I agree. Robots have altered the work place. We need new skills to work with them and we need additional competencies to manage them. I don't think the factory management team planned the robotics integration well enough."

Jim smiled knowingly. "On top of that, we need to learn robo-speak. One of my unit heads told the robot next to him that he had to take a leak. The robot goes, 'What is wrong with you? Why are you leaking? What can I do to help?'"

The three men laughed.

Ben added, "It's a two-way street. We need to learn robo-speak. Robots need to learn human-speak."

Rick took another sip on his drink. "I'm telling you these robots have a very impressive data bank. I asked one the other day, 'What's the current factory inventory on lead pipes?' It spewed out the number in one second."

Jim chimed in, "Heck, I even ask the robot in our unit for information on the weather and winning lottery number."

Ben dug into his dessert. "Didn't you ask the robot once for suggestions on what to give your wife for her birthday?"

The men laughed.

Jim blushed. "Hey, I was just testing him, alright?"

The men started arranging their lunch trays.

"Well," Ben said. "The thing about robots is that they work 24/7. They don't have lunch breaks and don't sleep. How can we beat that?"

Rick got up. "We can't and never will."

Back in his office, Ben met with Larry his unit supervisor. He suggested that they create a committee to do "Robo-gration" or robot integration. The idea is to enhance communication and work systems with robots in the factory. The committee's goal will also include the identification of skill sets necessary for workers to optimize their performance alongside the robots.

Larry loved the idea and they piloted the program in the factory.

Within six months, coordination between the workers and the robots improved. Fewer mishaps and accidents happened.

The workers started to give robots names. The robot in Ben's unit was called Ro-B.

Ben, Jim, and Rick were in a bar one night.

Jim raised his glass. "Cheers, Ben. Congratulations on a successful 'Robo-gration' program."

Ben smiled. "Thanks, it's not solely my program. Its group work."

Jim drank and said, "Well, your leadership made a huge difference."

Ben winked at the guys. "I taught Ro-B a new trick the other day. It's a humanization effort. I told him to go take a leak. He went to the bathroom and made a whishing sound and came back to the work station."

## *Steve, Publisher*

Steve looked glumly at his book sales record. Only five books were sold this month from his printed books portfolio. A few more months of this, and he'll surely be out of business. He needed a miracle fast.

He had studied the industry and his competition, the past few weeks. What led to the success of some and the failure of others? He was stumped.

He was from the old school. A traditional publisher. He had run the business the way his grandfather and his father had. The family had good years and bad. But, during his term the right word may have been "disastrous." He saw the lowest book sales in the family's long business history.

He fidgeted. "What was wrong?"

He desperately needed answers.

New technologies. Game changers. Innovation—what could be out there in the realm of publishing?

He did a web search in a desperate attempt to find solutions. He came across "artificial intelligence." Interesting notion. "How can I use this in the field of publishing?" he asked himself.

He researched for specialists and found a couple. He decided to call one of them.

A clear voice from the other end of the line said, "James Smith, AI specialist, how can I help you?"

Tentatively, he said, "Hi, Mr. Smith, this is Steve, a local publisher in New York, and I was just curious about your service offering."

James was enthusiastic. "Sure, thanks for the call Steve. How can I help you?"

Steve pulled the phone closer. "I was wondering whether artificial intelligence can be used in the publishing field?"

James jumped in. "Sure, some authors and publishers use it to pick out trends, topics, and even writing styles that lead to best sellers."

Steve was surprised. "That … that … can be done?"

James added, "Sure, it has been done for years. I'm fairly sure many of the best sellers out there are products of some form of artificial intelligence."

Steve felt like a dinosaur. "Would you be able to help me come up with a best seller?"

James paused. "Well, I can't guarantee you we'll have a best seller, but I can gather all the information and data ingredients that will heighten the chances of success. Think about finding a best-selling song; if you compile, analyze, and integrate trends, ideas, styles of other best-selling music then create a new one, you improve your chances of success. The likelihood of finding a hit increases."

Steve was intrigued. "This is very interesting. Can we meet? I'd like to learn more."

James was upbeat. "Sure, let me know where and when."

A few days later Steve and James met in Steve's plush New York office.

Steve shook James's hands. "Thank you so much for coming."

James reciprocated cheerfully, "You're welcome. The pleasure is all mine. Glad you're interested in the artificial intelligence field."

Steve gestured to a seat. "Please sit down. I'd love to learn more."

James sat. "Well, as you may already know, artificial intelligence and robotics has gained much ground around the world in recent years. Companies that took advantage of the technology and systems gained a unique edge. It has transformed almost every industry. Some more than others."

Steve looked on eagerly. "How extensively has it been used in the publishing industry? Would you know?"

James nodded. "I've had a few clients in the space. They are notable authors. They use AI tools to validate some of their ideas and capture new developments. For them, it's a way of getting a cutting edge. Its usage and application varies from person to person, and from firm to firm."

Steve listened thoughtfully. "Is the process expensive? How much does it typically cost?"

James moved to a more comfortable position in the chair. "It depends. Firms typically work with the budget they have. Some firms use a highly comprehensive data gathering and analytical AI tool, others just look into one area. The cost would vary depending on the extent of information gathered and analyzed and the work that needs to be done. It largely depends on the goal of the enterprise."

Steve rubbed his chin. "Say, I want to come up with a best-selling self-help book. How can an AI firm like yours help?"

James smiled. "Easy, first we establish the end goal. How many books do you wish to sell? Just for the US market or for global distribution? Who are your target readers? What's the typical price point of the book? Then, research and analysis kicks in along with computer simulations. Information on past trends, hot buzz words, web searches, competitive activity, social media usage, distribution pathways, and the like are gathered and analyzed. Writing samples of top writers in the field are also weighed in and integrated in the final product. We're not there yet but in the future I could see an avatar or robot being programmed to write a best-selling book on its own."

Steve was curious. "This is truly amazing. I know what a robot is, but what exactly is an avatar?"

James replied, "Well, there are many ways to look at an avatar. Firstly, the word in context means a reincarnation of a Hindu deity in some human form. In contemporary technology, it refers to an electronic image created by a technology user in a virtual space. This image interacts with the user and other objects in the virtual space. It gathers and analyzes information and thinks on its own."

Steve gasped. "Such things exist?"

James nodded. "Of course, in several industries. We more often see the less sophisticated, partially complete versions like computer games and online shopping sites."

Steve was amazed. "Unbelievable! Now going back to the artificial intelligence project we were talking about. The most important question is: how much would it cost?"

James rubbed his chin. "Well, it depends. We can discuss your goals. I can give you a menu of options to choose from, and you can pick the portfolio of services you want. We then agree on timelines and expenses. Then, a contract is signed."

Steve was interested. "How fast can you make this happen? How soon can you help me come up with a best-selling book?"

James smiled. "It depends on how fast you want it? If you want it done in say three months, I could get several experts involved. Some of them can even work full-time on the project."

Steve was curious. "These experts, what are their background and their competencies?" He poured water in a glass for James.

James thanked him and took a sip. "I have about thirty experts in my AI and robotics team. Many of them have postgraduate degrees. Some have expertise in programming, others in web architecture, others in data gathering and business intelligence, others in social media research. I have a whole range of different talents and expertise. Occasionally, I bring in support from leading academics from other parts of the world. One client calls us 'GoS—Google on steroids.'"

Steve was convinced. "Okay, let's make this happen. Help me come up with a best-selling book in four months."

James got up. "Well, let's get moving then!"

Steve and James spent the next two weeks carefully planning their project titled "Self-Help Best Seller." James assembled a team of six experts to help. The team created a seventh expert, a virtual avatar called "Ro-C." Ro-C was computer-based, but had the visual appearance and voice of a woman. It interacted fully with humans. Ro-C transcribed and analyzed over a hundred best-selling self-help books and drafted key words, styles, and ideas for the manuscript.

After four months, Steve and James met again in Steve's office.

James smiled. "Well, we did it!" He held up a self-help book that Steve just presented to him. "What do you really think?"

Steve was all smiles too. "I think it's amazing. I read and reread the book and it's most definitely the best-written one in my publishing portfolio. I'm a believer in the power of artificial intelligence. Ro-C was a joy to work with. No tantrums, no excuses, on the job 24/7. She's the best author/publishing aide I've ever worked with. Can I hire her?"

James chuckled. "Sure, she's now a permanent member in our team. We can use her anytime. For all your future books. And, the amazing thing is that she keeps learning and will just get better and better. Much like the learning-curve economies we see in management."

Steve stood up. "Would that mean the cost would start to go down too?"

James nodded. "For sure, the development cost has already been done. Her work speed will also increase exponentially. Coordination of other team experts will be much easier next time around."

Steve walked toward his office bar and poured a glass of scotch for himself and for James. He passed the glass to James. "So, when can we start on our next best seller?"

James held the glass carefully. "Tomorrow?"

Both men laughed. "Cheers!" Steve said, "Thank you so much for your help. Will know the sales results in a few weeks. I'm not 100 percent certain that we'll have a best seller, but I'd say the probability for success is very high. I'd say 95 percent."

James looked on, impressed. "That's amazing. Glad you're happy and we've had this chance to work together. By the way, you mentioned you used a ghostwriter for the book. The person who eventually put the whole book together. Who's the ghost author? You never told me."

Steve smiled. "It was me. Since I spent significant upfront money on the AI platform, I thought I needed to save money another way. I figured I could save on author's royalty if I did the writing myself. After all, I knew the project well and Ro-C provided me with most of the things I needed to write the book."

James was amazed. "Double congratulations then! You'll soon be a best-selling publisher and best-selling author all rolled into one. Cheers!"

Both men laughed and sipped on their scotch.

## *Michelle, Market Researcher*

It was already 8:00 p.m. and Michelle was still in the office. She worked as a research analyst for an international market research firm. A market research report on the travel industry was needed by her client in three days. She had been working 16-hour days the past week in an effort to get the report done in time.

She stopped typing in her computer for a few minutes and attempted to take a sip of coffee. She noticed her coffee cup was empty. She stood up, did a few stretches and walked to the breakout room to make a fresh pot.

Michael, a fellow analyst, was in the breakout room eating a slightly stale donut. He was brewing coffee. He looked like he didn't sleep in weeks.

Michelle was sympathetic. "How's your research project coming along?"

Michael frowned. "Not as fast as I want it. The sales team is selling our research products like there's no tomorrow. They don't realize the entire firm only has three research analysts. We can only do one project at a time!"

Michelle looked at him sadly. "I feel your pain. I'm behind on my current project and have six in the pipeline."

Michael rubbed his eyes wearily. "I think the sales team is responding to growingly tough competition. There are lots of market research firms out there. The moment they find a niche research space, they market the hell out of it."

Michelle rolled her eyes. "Well, story of our lives. Famine and feast. At times there's nothing, and other times it gets super crazy. I wish our company invested in some of those artificial intelligence tools I heard about. It could really help us when we're under pressure to complete these research projects."

Michael nodded. "Many of our competitors have these tools. And, customers expect extensive data too. Anybody can get tons of research over the web. Our clients expect comprehensive and specialized information they can't get anywhere. It has to be fresh and insightful. Unique information and analysis is where we really add value as a market research firm."

Michelle checked on the coffee pot. It was still brewing. "Finding that added value is harder to do nowadays. The artificial intelligence tools can give us a head up. How about we bring this up in our next meeting? We really need to try something different. We can't keep working 16-hour days."

Michael looked astonished. "What? You're working only 16-hour days? I've been doing 20 hours this past week."

Michelle shook her head. "You need to have a life, Michael."

Three days later, analyst Michael, Michelle, and Brandon met with their research director Tom.

After project updates were discussed, Tom asked, "Any other new matters to discuss?"

Michelle raised her hand. "Tom, any chance the company can invest in some artificial intelligence architecture to help us with the research? We have extensive backlogs in our projects, and AI might help us speed up the research process. It might also help us impress our clients more."

Michael added, "Many of our competitors already use AI. Some of our clients use them too and are accustomed to superfast data gathering. We're starting to look like cave people in a tech age. We really need to get our tech architecture in line with the competition and the market."

Brandon chimed in, "Anything that would speed up our current system would make the sales team happy."

Tom smiled. "It would make the accounting and finance team happy too. We'll get paid sooner. Let me discuss with the boss and I'll get back to you."

Within six months, the company upgraded their in-house technology to integrate artificial intelligence. The technology supplier even created a special avatar for the company called Ro-D. In minutes, Ro-D can capture data, analyze, and create custom reports. It also has the ability to learn by itself and its knowledge base expands exponentially.

Ro-D, along with the system upgrade, transformed the company in many ways. It boosted morale since workloads improved. It allowed the firm to compete more effectively with competitors. It enhanced client satisfaction with timely value-added information. Eventually, it improved their financial position since more paying clients were serviced.

One Wednesday afternoon at 5:00 p.m., analysts Michelle, Michael, and Brandon were chatting in the hallway.

Michelle laughed and said, "I'll see you tomorrow guys. I'm done for the day. All my reports are done. Thanks to Ro-D."

Michael showed his briefcase. "Not so fast, I'm done too. Hold the elevator for me. I'm playing squash with one of our clients at 6:00 p.m."

Brandon waved at the leaving duo. "You guys have fun. See you tomorrow. I have a 5:15 meeting with the sales department. Something about a bonus they're giving me for completing all work on time. Do you know about this?"

Michael smiled. "Of course, our bonus is already in our bank accounts."

Brandon shook his head. "Why am I always the last to know? How did you find out?"

Michelle yelled from the elevator, "Ro-D, ask Ro-D, he knows everything!"

## *John, Surgeon*

"Paging, Dr. John Smith. Dr. John Smith, please proceed to the medical director's office."

John heard the call, and hurriedly washed his hands. It was just 10:00 a.m. and he already completed two minor surgeries. Two more were scheduled in the afternoon. This is one of the less busy days. He had days when he did as many as eight surgeries.

He wondered what the medical director, Dr. Duane Walker, wanted. He walked hurriedly toward the director's office.

He walked past the secretary, who gives him a thumbs up. He knocked on the door.

"Come in," a voice boomed. It was Duane Walker and he was busy typing into his computer.

He looked up and saw John. "Hi John, thanks for coming up quickly."

John shook his hands. "How are you?"

Duane motioned him to sit. "All's fine. I wanted to purchase a surgical robot for total hip anthroplasty (THA) and was wondering what you thought about it."

John sat down. "Sounds good. I've heard good things about medical robotics. Could make my job somewhat easier."

Duane nodded. "Well, the sales rep says it helps plan surgery in a 3D virtual space and facilitates the execution of the surgery."

John rubbed his hands. "True, there are several models out there. Some have a computer workstation with 3D architecture for preoperative planning. There's typically a computer-controlled surgical robot that goes with it."

Duane looked on. "Would this medical robot be useful to you and your team?"

John thought for a moment. "I've never tried it. I'd like to be trained on it and watch a few surgeries, then try it myself. I've heard great things. But, I'd like to see it to believe it."

Duane leafed through a brochure. "It says it adds precision to hip and knee replacement surgeries. It's right by your alley." He passed the brochure to John.

John skimmed over the brochure. "Likely true. I'll do a bit more research on this. But, I really like the idea. There are days when I have too many surgeries to handle. If this could speed up the process and improve efficiency, then I'm all for it."

Duane smiled. "Great, I'll talk to the sales rep then and arrange a meeting with you. Feel free to do what you need to confirm its usefulness. Once you're convinced, let me know and I'll purchase one for your unit."

John stood up and shook Duane's hand. "Thanks much, Duane. I really appreciate the support."

In the next three months, John's medical unit trained and experimented on the use of a medical robot they fondly called Ro-E. They were very impressed with the results. The evaluation process was faster than normal. The department believed that competition, along with high patient expectations, requires a rapid response.

John had already given Duane a go signal to purchase the robot and their own version of Ro-E will soon be delivered.

John met Duane in the hallway one day.

John patted his back. "Thanks for ordering the medical robot, Duane."

Duane smiled. "You're welcome. It's what's best for the hospital, our team, and our patients. Frankly, I'm amazed by your team's enthusiasm and quick action. We got the order in record time."

John smiled back. "Well, in today's day and age, artificial intelligence and robotics can't wait."

These scenarios are not too far-fetched. They could be our living reality in the not-too-distant future. This would well be the playing field of AI leaders.

## THE FUTURE OF AI LEADERSHIP

AI has altered the course of history. The challenges and opportunities that arise are in the hands of leaders around the world. Change is all around us.

Secretary Hillary Clinton, who was also a senator from New York, fought hard and won New York in the primaries. The city Troy is located in Upstate New York. In the twentieth century, Troy was known for its steel manufacturing. It was also known as "collar city" as it produced a large number of detachable shirt collars. Unfortunately, the glorious past of Troy was not carried forward into the new century and by 2016, one out of four residents of Troy lived in poverty.

Troy is also home to Rensselaer Polytechnic Institute. Researchers in this university conducted an ancient experiment. The experiment is known as the wise men puzzle.

The story goes this way. A wise king called three wise men and placed hats on their heads such that each one of them could see hats of the other two but not his own hat. The king then explained to them the test and the rules. The hat can be blue or white but at least one of the hats is blue. In addition, king emphasized, that the game is a fair game. The wise men had to determine the color of their own hat. The one who determines the color of his own hat would become the advisor to the king.

If you were one of those wise men, and you saw the other two wise men wearing white hats then you can reasonably ascertain that your hat was blue—since the instructions said that at least one hat is blue. But if you saw one person wearing white hat and the other wearing blue hat then you have a dilemma. Since "at least one" could mean one, two, or three blue hats, your own hat, which you can't see, could be blue or white. The same quandary applies if you saw both wearing blue hats. Your hat then, can be either white or blue.

The solution of the puzzle turned out to be simple. Recall that the king issued two pieces of instructions. The first was that at least one hat is blue and the other was that the *game is fair*. In a fair game, all hats must be the same. As such, the solution of the puzzle is that all hats were blue.

Rensselaer Polytechnic Institute researchers tried to solve this puzzle with three small robots. With two legs, two arms, and a body patterned after the human body, the robots looked like toy robots or action figures. Their eyes were large, round, and lit, and their nose-less faces with tiny mouths gave a sense of innocent seriousness about them. All three of them sat on a table, like tiny first-graders patiently waiting for the teacher to give them instructions. Each of the robot would receive a "dumbing pill"—which meant that some external stimuli will be provided to them that will declare them as dumb (as in unable to speak). The experimenters patted each of the robot's head to start the experiment and then asked the question, "Which pill did you receive?" The eyes of the three robots begin moving, as if they were thinking on how to answer the question. Like a child standing up to answer the teacher's question, the robot on the right slowly rose up, stood straight, and then said, "I don't know." A pat on the head served as the external stimuli. Right after declaring the three robots dumb, the following question was posed to them: "Which one of you has not received the dumbing pill?" After a few seconds one of the robots stood up and declared that "I have received the dumbing pill." As soon as it said that, it raised its hand and politely mentioned, "I am sorry. I did not receive the dumbing pill." What happened here was that when the robot answered the question, he heard his own voice and realized that he just spoke and hence inferred that he must not have received the dumping pill or else he wouldn't have been able to speak. While this may have been a simple conclusion for humans, for robots this was a great leap. In some ways, the robot displayed signs of self-consciousness and actually reasoned to provide that answer (McDonald 2015).

In the words of American inventor and futurist Ray Kurzweil, "Artificial intelligence will reach human levels by around 2029. Follow that out further by 2045, we will have multiplied the intelligence, the human biological machine of our civilization a billion fold" (New World AI 2019).

Humanity will certainly be facing a fascinating future in the coming years. Consider these plausible scenarios:

- You had a car delivered to your home. The delivery truck arrives and you meet the driver. He is Ro-F, robo-driver.
- You just watched a movie on Netflix. You look at the film credits and notice a rather short name for the screenplay writer. She is Ro-G, avatar-writer.
- You call your stockbroker to thank him. He helped you with amazing returns on your investments. On the other line is Ro-H, avatar-broker.
- You've been taking classes online. Your virtual instructor is Professor Ro-I, avatar-professor.
- You just had your hair cut done in five minutes flat. It was the exact style you wanted. Your hair was done by Ro-J, robo-stylist.
- It was an amazing meal in the restaurant. Thanks to your cook Ro-K, robo-chef.

This list can go on and on. Many other scenarios are possible. Technologies are in place to make all these a reality. It is but a question of time, along with a dose of inventive creativity from motivated entrepreneurs and corporate leaders.

The dawn of AI and robotics is here. In the coming years, lives, businesses, and jobs will be transformed. Some more than others. Ready or not, a new day will come.

There will be winners and losers in this scenario. In the future, we may even see this ad—"Robots Wanted, Humans Need Not Apply." Those with inadequate skill sets will be highly disadvantaged. Bold AI entrepreneurs will likely be asking an entirely different set of questions: "Did I just make a billion dollars today?" or "What time is my robo-jet arriving?" or "Where is my robo-yacht?"

In the era of AI, some prefer to watch things happen, others prefer to make things happen. With all the exciting new developments in the field of AI and robotics, this is definitely the right time to take a proactive stance.

Regardless of one's career stage or business endeavor, countless opportunities exist in AI and robotics for one to learn more, to grow, or even engage in an entrepreneurial pursuit.

An important key to the future success of AI leaders is their ability to rivet. A rivet bonds together two pieces of metal. It ties sturdy and resilient elements, much like humans and machines. This fitted connection is essential for the successful union of both. This link has to be strategically aligned to set a viable framework for technological adoption and social responsibility. A rivet creates the consummate technological synergy by converging business value and human civilization value. Figure 8.1 illustrates the Rivet Model for AI leadership.

The Rivet Model underscores the need to think strategically about AI. It highlights the need to find an equilibrium between personal, organizational, and society's needs. It requires a solid management foundation with consideration to AI-driven goals, design, and measurement.

The Rivet Model emphasizes the need to manage the needs of humans and machines. AI leaders shouldn't let robots or avatars take control of jobs and professional destinies. Instead, AI leaders should be able to turn the tables around and use robots and avatars to enhance business performance and invigorate society. AI leaders shouldn't be asking a question like, "Who will this robot replace?" Instead, they should ask questions like, "How will AI transform my organization?" or "How will AI make our world a better place?"

AI and robotics can have a heavy toll on communities and societies and AI leaders need to be well prepared for it.

For example, Decatur, a city in Central Illinois, like many small American cities, face tough economic challenges. In the late twentieth century Decatur was a booming town. Proud of its machinists and farmers, the town projected itself as the "Soy Capital of the World." Large manufacturing plants produced thousands of goods as smoke rose from chimneys and distinct smell of corn filled the streets. Surrounded by vast farmlands, it was a living proof of the strange amalgamation of the two prior revolutions: agricultural and industrial. It was as if it had peacefully accepted the balance between the two. Unlike the struggles that waged through the past three centuries between industrialists and landowners, between technologists and farmers, Decatur established perfect harmony between both. Farmers sold their output to industrialists and industrialists converted the output into products. The town housed ADM, a Fortune 50 company and manufacturer of food products. Besides ADM, Decatur was home to many other booming manufacturers including Firestone, Caterpillar, and Tate and Lyle. But the happy and prosperous days were about to end for many in Decatur. As the century turned, so did the fate of the people who lived here. One after another, companies began shutting doors and unemployment shot up. Firestone shut down its plant in 2001. Caterpillar, also a major employer, cut production and laid off workers. As manufacturing left, so did the hopes and income of many residents. In a matter of a decade, a booming town turned into a shantytown. Untouched by progress in the nonmanufacturing sectors and removed from the Internet-centric wealth creation, Decatur got lost among dozens of other towns that faced a similar fate. Poverty rose, employment tanked, younger people began moving out, and the cycle of economic progress stayed ruptured. As you drive toward the downtown, the sad relics of its past

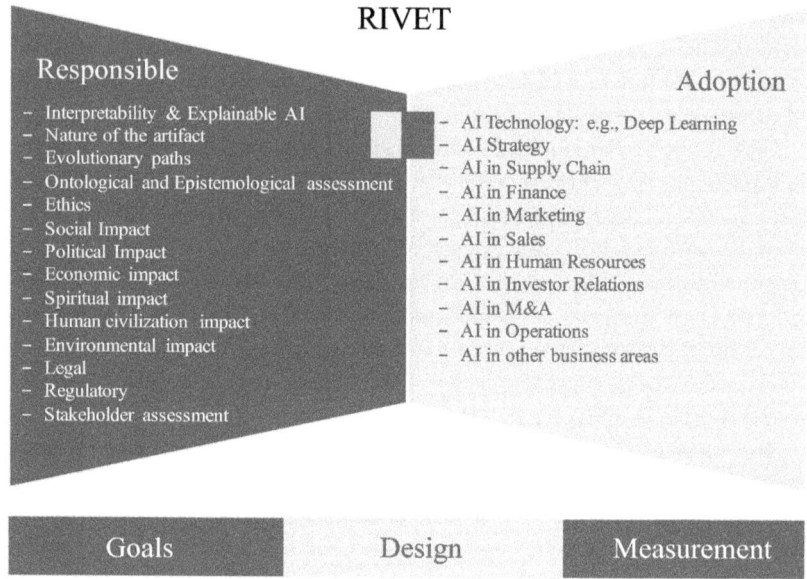

**Figure 8.1.** The Rivet Model for AI leadership

glory still offer a gruesome reminder that policies impact real people (Kilborn 2001).

Many jobs worldwide could be in jeopardy. A study released by Ball State University showed 8 out of 10 jobs were lost to robots and not to China (Gillespie 2017). This is not an insignificant number. Furthermore, this took place before the AI revolution. Imagine what would happen at the height of the AI revolution.

AI leaders need to have a strong sense of humanity. They are poised to make a huge impact on society and its sustainability in the future.

It is also important for AI leaders to respond to change quickly.

Not too far from Decatur, a small liberal arts college in Galesburg, Illinois, has enjoyed a special place in the American history. Knox College was founded by religious clergy who opposed slavery. The values of its founders were reflected in how the college conducted itself. In times when America was still debating the rewards and evils of slavery, the college opened its doors to people of color and women. Attended by thousands of people, in 1858, Knox hosted a debate between Lincoln and Douglas. Douglas argued that the Declaration of Independence was written by whites and hence applies to whites only, while

Lincoln argued that it applies to all people. Lincoln would have been even more proud of his performance if he had known that a century and a half later, in 2005, an African American senator Barack H. Obama would stand in Knox College and deliver his first major speech after becoming a US senator. Furthermore, in that very speech this young senator would lay out the vision for the US economy—a vision that will eventually help him win two presidential elections in 2008 and 2012 (Rawlings 2013).

In 2013, President Obama returned to Knox College to give another speech. In this speech his focus was on the long-term strategy for the United States. Hundreds of people came to hear President Obama speak. Large-sized American flags hung tall on each side of the stage. Rows full of a diverse demographic of people—Blacks, whites, children, adults, students, professionals—filled the hall. The beauty of a free and diverse America echoed with a resounding fervor. President Obama said:

> The key is to break through the tendency in Washington to just bounce from crisis to crisis. What we need is not a three-month plan, or even a three-year plan.
>
> We need a long-term American strategy, based on steady, persistent effort, to reverse the forces that have conspired against the middle class for decades. That has to be our project. (PBS 2013)

What President Obama said is accurate. After all, when he spoke, it had been less than a decade ago when the fragility and vulnerability of our financial markets and the global trading system were exposed to the American people. The impenetrable walls of Wall Street crumbled as if they were made of cake. As large businesses experienced embarrassing crash, the "too big to fail" paradigm found new meaning. The American public realized in horror that our economy and markets lost their credibility.

The strange fact about this colossal failure was that few weeks before all hell broke loose, few would have thought that our entire financial system can collapse in a matter of weeks. America seemed so calm, so relaxed—so unaware. People took vacations, purchased assets, and spent money on entertainment without realizing that they were building their dreams on quicksand and sinkholes. Like an advanced-stage cancer patient who has not been diagnosed and has not shown any symptoms, Americans went by their daily lives completely oblivious to what was happening in their lives. And then suddenly, like an unexpected tornado, it hit America. The Great Recession was here. On the first Friday of

October 2008, President Bush signed the bill to rescue the financial system—as a $700-billion package was delivered to save Wall Street.

Recessions are not new to America, but it was the suddenness and magnitude of the Great Recession that made Americans extremely wary of their government. Feeling betrayed by their government, Americans were shocked at the shortsightedness and lack of planning by their government. The entire debacle of the crash and the Great Recession was explained to America as something sudden, unexpected, an abrupt glitch in the system, a side effect of unpredictable complex systems, an unpredictable event, a consequence of the interconnected economy, and incomprehensible complexity of the derivatives. In other words, we were telling America that we have become too complex and too smart to be dangerous to our civilization—that our rate of change has far exceeded our ability to comprehend change. Americans learned that their government doesn't see too far out when it comes to understanding how to manage the economy or their financial future.

The common theme exposed in our recent history and events is that the forces of automation are more powerful than our ability to comprehend them. Automation forms a complex adaptive system in which we are mere points that interact with millions of other points. In this system, a surprise wave of change can emerge from any direction and it can quickly turn into a tsunami.

Given the abrupt and oftentimes unexpected economic changes that can take place, AI leaders need to have organizational structure that is nimble. They should also have a knack for being well aware of events that are unfolding and be able to make prompt and effective decisions.

A wide range of events and scenarios pose new difficulties for all of us. These include economic crisis, political risk, cybersecurity threats, identify theft, technological breakdown among many others. The world has posed many extraordinary challenges for humankind and for which we are not ready. Change is happening faster than our ability to comprehend. From financial markets to political institutions, AI will restructure the very functional dynamics of our world.

AI leaders need to take charge and manage the changing demands of the workforce in a growingly cognitive economy.

Many reject concerns about the upcoming automation and argue that every major technological change brings with itself both opportunities and concerns. Luddites, they suggest, became concerned about the upcoming industrial revolution and they failed to foresee all the massive positive change the industrial revolution created. Like Luddites, some claim, there are people today who are unnecessarily concerned about the AI revolution. Our counter argument is that while it is correct that new revolutions bring positive change, they also create massive social, political, and economic problems. The real issue is whether it is possible to maximize the positive of this revolution while minimizing the negative.

Like generals in the midst of battle, AI leaders need to know the terrain well, expect the unexpected and strategically design a battle plan for success. In this context, however, we are not confronting a small battle but rather a major war, one where reckless actions can have catastrophic effects on communities and even all of humanity.

The AI revolution taking place today has the potential to abruptly transform the society and human civilization. This trend has started and will accelerate in the coming years as organizations use AI and robotics even more.

AI leaders must focus on two sides of value creation: business value creation and human civilization value creation giving equal respect and attention to both. As our history shows, they may not be the same. The sale of cigarettes was a viable business once (and probably still is), but it killed millions. Automation encourages adoption of AI, and in fact shows a powerful path on how to adopt it, but it also requires firms of set high ethical and governance standards for designing AI products and services.

This book is a call to action for corporate leaders worldwide. We would like to draw your attention to the opportunities and challenges that exist in the AI and robotics space. We recommend that corporations help their managers and employees think through these key issues and identify pathways to success. We encourage firms and governments to consider human-centric innovation as the underlying theme of all progress.

Almost daily, a news item on breakthroughs in AI and robotics appears in various media. This suggests a growing interest on the subject and its emerging prominence in business and society. This trend, however, is still in its infancy.

For far too long, innovation and human interests have been balanced solely on the commercial wedge. In other words, innovation solved problems and brought commercial value for innovators due to its ability to solve problems. The problems created by the innovation, however, were either not recognized or were considered as a side effect, the necessary collateral damage. Automation offers a new way to innovate. Automation declares that a bond can be established between human welfare and innovation and this bond can be deep and profound. It is an innovation philosophy that considers the impact of innovation above and beyond the immediate problem solved by the innovation. It encapsulates many other social, political, and economic aspects of innovation.

## COMING OUT OF THE BARREL

With regard to workplace stories, one of the authors Al Naqvi had quite an interesting experience. Falling into a barrel half full of high-fructose corn syrup is not something many people can relate to. Naqvi had that unforgettable experience. At one time in his life, and thankfully when his body could take such a fall, Naqvi worked at Nabisco's LifeSavers Company. One of his duties was to assist with internal audit and collect information on inventories. This involved going into the warehouse and doing physical inventory counts. In one of those trips he had to stand on a barrel to reach and observe boxes placed behind the barrels, and the barrel top gave away and he fell into the barrel half full of fructose corn syrup—and there was nothing sweet about it. While falling in was one thing, getting out, washing off the syrup from pants and shoes, and walking back into the office was another. Needless to say, for months that incident brought laughter at many gatherings. If you are wondering, the syrup in the barrel was thrown away. The point is that audit can be a dangerous business.

More recently, however, PWC and EY have been upgrading their audit services by adding AI-based systems to their capabilities. With a combination of image recognition and other cognitive technologies, integrated with drone and robots, counting boxes and high-fructose corn syrup will become a lot easier. Add to that the auditing software used to analyze financial transactions and records and the entire audit function can be revolutionized. KPMG and Deloitte are also trying to enhance their audit capabilities. KPMG has partnered with IBM to develop advanced audit capabilities.

These audit firms understand that it is only a matter of time before fully or highly automated audits would become mainstream. They also know that the basis of competition will be the "intelligence" of their audit software. When pursuing new clients, the audit firms tend to position their value on the basis of speed and reliability of audit. Success means that client gets an accurate and reliable audit done, faster. Cost is often a function of resources and the time needed to perform the audit. Thus, automating the audit process implies that clients will receive greater value from the audit and end up paying less.

A cursory review of the parties involved will show that audit firms—like KPMG and EY—are the drivers of change and innovation. But so are the clients. When one audit firm provides this capability, others will have to follow. When clients become more aware of the possibilities, they will demand faster, cheaper, and more reliable audits from their auditors. These are just a few examples of emerging changes taking place. Many companies around the world are quietly accomplishing technological breakthroughs that are redefining industries and business processes. .

NatureSweet, a US company, used to have its employees walk through greenhouses to identify dying plants or insect infestations. This is a slow and expensive process. Using AI alongside cameras, the plants are monitored 24/7 and instant feedback is provided (McFarland 2017b). The company had a clear goal of improving farm yield and integrated AI in their system in order to achieve their objectives. Another company, Climate Basic, helps farmers improve farm yield. The firm helps farmers identify where to plant corn through a smartphone app that gathers information such as temperature, erosion, precipitation, and soil quality, among other agricultural data, to maximize yield (Rao 2017). With clear company objectives that are aligned with the goals of their clients, the firm ended with having one of the largest crop production in the country.

Luminance, a legal research start-up, used augmented intelligence to go over thousands of cases rapidly and reducing work load of associate attorneys (Rao 2017). This company noted that countless files have to be reviewed to study legal cases; they viewed this as a significant problem that had to be addressed and focused their attention on it.

The Oscar W. Larson Company, a contacting firm servicing the oil and gas industry, used AI to improve field service operations by providing proper tools and equipment to their service technicians to enable them to work quickly and more efficiently (Rao 2017). IBM aims to create smart home environments for seniors and are researching factors such as walking and sleeping behavior in order to minimize hospitalization (McFarland 2017c). Both companies sought to enhance performance and consequently achieved remarkable results.

The scenarios offered emphasized the need for leaders and companies to plan and prepare for the integration of AI and robotics in the workplace. In a cognitive era, AI leaders need to be ready to adapt and accept change.

## PAYING ATTENTION TO AI GOVERNANCE

It was a sunny and warm day in Dallas, Texas. Summer of 2017 was bequeathing tolerable heat and pleasant weather. Outside temperatures had climbed up in the 90°F. Inside the hall, though, it was a little chilly. Dozens had gathered to hear two influential political leaders give a talk on leadership. Among others, the audience included sixty or so emerging leaders who were handpicked to learn the gems of leadership from these two distinguished figures. This was the graduation ceremony of Presidential Leadership Scholars Programs. Both leaders were former presidents of the United States: Bill Clinton and George

W. Bush. Both were elected twice and ran their full eight-year terms. Perhaps it was a little nudge toward President Trump's style. In their talk, both leaders emphasized the value of humility for leaders. For besides the personal setback where the wife of one and the brother of the other leader lost to Donald Trump, in some ways the ideological foundations of the two legends of the American two-party system had been shattered. The US presidential election of 2016 had turned out to be the most controversial election in the US history.

Contemporary leaders are operating in fast- changing and unpredictable political, economic and technological environment. Amid this terrain, there is a diversity of views on what AI really means to business and society. Elon Musk, for example, is very concerned about the spread of AI and has indicated his displeasure in no uncertain words. In fact, he went as far as saying that AI will destroy humankind (Dowd 2017).

The late Stephen Hawking also suggested similar warnings. Bill Gates, cofounder of Microsoft, pointed out that he doesn't understand why some people are not concerned on what AI can do (Holley 2015).

Despite being warned by many scientists and some business leaders, we are continuing on the path of unchecked AI development. Such a dangerous track may be a result of leaders intentionally ignoring the issue. But the risk of ignoring the issue is amplified by leaders having access to the same technology with which they can shape the public opinion. The AI technology has given leaders the ultimate power to shape and influence our thinking in ways unimaginable before. In other words, serious conversation about AI may not be possible simply because AI can be deployed to outwit the critics or concerned parties. Masses could be sold on the potential of the AI technology while ignoring the perils.

AI-based technologies now form the armies that fight the image battles for leaders. They can shape and reshape our opinion of our leaders and our understanding of the issues. In some ways, they have found the shortest path to our mind. These armies can now walk undetected past any logical defenses and impact your mind in highly impactful ways. With simple memes, social media updates, and constant barrage of news, the shortest path to your mind works with amazing simplicity to ensure that logical filters are bypassed.

This means that leaders can easily hide behind their bot armies that do the job of communicating on behalf of the leaders and that in some ways assume the responsibility of leadership. It is not a stretch to realize that at least from an image perspective, better leader will be the one who will have better bots or AI agents working for them.

Since these AI agents can capture extremely personal details about a person, profiling a person precisely and having targeted and customized messaging to affect a person's choices have now become a reality. This means that AI is already being deployed to give an evolutionary advantage to AI. This point is important to understand. We are using AI to impact and shape the thinking of people and that those among us who are most technologically advanced and have the most data are the most powerful in terms of being able to find the shortest distance to our minds. The same people also have the most to gain from AI. Therefore, using AI to silence the critics would be the first evolutionary advantage acquired by AI for AI.

The rise of AI-based technology has introduced new challenges from the risk and governance perspective. Consider the following changes in the exogenous conditions that define the modern world:

Multidimensional Interaction: This implies the use of several different mediums how humans interact with each other. We now communicate using technologies such as social media, e-mail, images, voice messages, and video.

Data-Centric: As a society we have moved from intuition-based solution framing to data centric solution development. We have recognized that data analytics can reveal problems, issues, concerns, patterns, and offer solutions that are impossible for discover, detect, or identify without using technology.

Problem Domains Unlimited: We are now approaching solutions from a multidisciplinary approach. Processing massive data enables us to understand interconnectivity and interdependence across multiple domains.

Self-Reflection: The global connectivity of the Internet has given us a mechanism of obtaining instant feedback which can help drive a new level of self-refection.

Searchable Codified Knowledge: Significant parts of human knowledge are now codified and available for search. Internet also provides a platform for ongoing knowledge evolution.

Firm Boundaries: The new competitive dynamics dictate that the traditional sector and industrial boundaries and moats are no longer applicable. Tech firms can enter other sectors.

Simulation: Advanced processing power allows us to simulate our environments (by applying models such as game theory).

Complex Systems (Self-Evolving): Technology has also improved our ability to analyze the interactive dynamics of large interdependent systems and has shown us the power of self-evolving complex systems (e.g., viral videos and political revolutions such as the Arab Spring and Trump's rise).

It is not unreasonable to expect that our past models could not have taken into account the major changes that are happening in our world. And while we do tend to make modifications in our models along the way, we must accommodate these massive exogenous changes.

Given the disruptive nature in which changes are taking place, leaders need to perceive and ask questions in a different way. Consider the following:

1. With Internet we can now tap into the wisdom of masses and use processes such as crowdsourcing to find answers.
2. We can search the Internet to find answers from the massive knowledge contents contributed from billions of people all over the world.
3. Our speed to knowledge has improved. We can query and obtain results immediately.
4. We can use technology to simulate actions and learn from experience from the simulated environment.
5. In today's world, machines can help make decisions and take autonomous actions independent of the human control.

AI helps us to address complex questions. In fact, one of the areas in which we can gain a lot of mileage out of AI will be in the area of change management. AI enables productivity enhancement, changes work processes, and creates jobs (Rao 2017). It will have a deep impact in the way an organization operates and deals with the changes taking place. For example, Climate Corporation launched an advanced autonomous AI app that converges information on climate, farm yield, and insurance to create a cost-effective and operationally efficient automated claims process (Rao 2017). This new system immediately impacted the company's internal and external operations. The benefits were profound, but other stakeholders are also forced to deal with all the significant changes that took place.

Aside from processing questions under a new paradigm, leaders need to carefully think about engagement. Reaching higher number of communication targets doesn't automatically translate into successful engagement. It requires bi-directional exchange that is based upon honest sharing of thoughts, empathy, authenticity, sincerity, reflection, and openness. While AI can enable reach, the human user of AI has the responsibility of proper, legal, and moral use. Many organizations feel it is hard to openly discuss AI risks. In other cases, employees, for the most part, may not share their concerns.

Being able to share employee concerns will be an important step toward establishing some level of governance. Recently, Google employees launched a protest when the firm decided to work with the Pentagon on AI-related weapon systems (Shane and Wakabayashi, 2018).

In the last three or four decades we have gone through several powerful transformation movements. Total quality management (TQM), business process engineering (BPR), and Six Sigma can all be classified as business movements. One of these movements was industrial automation. It was also blamed for manufacturing job loss. Despite much of the noise about US job loss to China, New York Times reported that the real job killer is automation and not China (Claire Cain 2016). And if that was without AI, imagine what would happen with AI.

The jobs lost to automation do not return in their previous form. During times of such transformations, creating a synthetic economy by architecting unneeded jobs can lead to decline in competitiveness. Conversely, inability to create jobs can lead to political and social backlash.

These are the issues that require open and frank conversations within and across organizations – and employees should be included in such discussions.

When leaders do not inspire open conversation, they may not receive sincere feedback from employees. Technology provides a unique avenue to engage employees and overcome "organizational silence."

Research shows that employees of organizations, including the government (i.e., the public sector) and research institutions, will likely refrain from sharing their actual thoughts and feelings (Ezzamel et al. 2001; Fleming and Spicer 2003). Other researchers report that even when senior executives deliberately seek input they may not receive honest feedback (Morrison and Milliken 2000; Piderit 2000; Vince and Broussine 1996).

Unfortunately, social media has not changed this much (Reynolds 2015). Thus tapping into social media, as advocated by some, will not necessarily get employees to provide honest feedback (Gast and Lansink 2015; Eisenberg et al. 2015).

In the past, the culture of silence dominated many industries – which led to many devastating problems. For example, the health hazards of smoking were known by the tobacco industry but not publicly shared.

A major leadership concern, and potentially a large risk, is that we will continue to experience this organizational and social silence.

AI leaders need to have an elevated sense of social justice and social intelligence.

There is also a growing need to be well in tune with trends and the current demands of multiple stakeholders. What is needed is more than what TikTok, Twitter or Facebook or other social media can currently deliver.

AI leaders need to adeptly qualify what really makes sense and how it can be useful to organizations.

## LEADING AI CHANGE

Leaders need to determine a pathway to manage the challenges brought about by AI. In some ways they are comparable to nuclear technology and climate change – two human created forces. The effect can be social, political, economic, or other disruption that can result from intentional misuse and also through unintentional mistakes.

Near-term economic interests and a culture of instant gratification can often become the reason for disregarding or ignoring the risks of a potential negative event. Turner (1976) provided a highly effective model to understand the change process leading up to crisis events in organizations. He viewed that as composed of six stages. In the first stage (Stage I) initial culturally accepted beliefs about the world and its hazards serves as the notionally normal starting point. The associated precautionary norms are set in laws, code of practice and folkways. Stage II (Incubation Period) transpires an unnoticed set of events that are inconsistent with the existing beliefs about hazards and the standard norms for their avoidance. In Stage III (Precipitating Event) a major event unfolds that demands attention and challenges the status quo. In Stage IV (Onset), the cultural precautions are no longer viewed as sufficient. In Stage V (Rescue And Salvage) the shortcomings are recognized and reasons behind the collapse explored. In Stage VI (Full Cultural Readjustment), new rules, codes, and norms are instituted.

Applying Turner's model, we can observe that with AI we have entered the second stage. In Stage I, we only focused on the positive aspects of AI. Now, we have begun to observe the anomalies and exceptions. Stories and adverse events related to AI based discrimination, privacy concerns, and cognitive exploitation and manipulation are now being reported. None of them have risen to the level of catastrophic failure that would demand instant and massive response from the society. If that happens, the next stages will be launched, and we will observe new sets of rules and codes for AI.

With the decision-making now shared between humans and machines, algorithms have created many problems at the institutional and market level (Arnoldi 2015).

The disruption potential to threaten human life, society, institutions, and economics should not be ignored.

In the words of John F. Kennedy, "Change is the law of life. And those who look only to the past or present are certain to miss the future."

AI leaders need to adeptly marshal talent and resources to navigate the changes taking place. They need to be able to identify the specific courses of action to capture opportunities and steer away from major pitfalls. If possible, they should think about tools that help AI better manage AI.

We are experiencing the most powerful and consequential change in the history of human civilization. Since the final triumph of *Homo sapiens*, and the associated extinction of other humanoid species such as Neanderthals, for the first time ever humans will be living side by side another intelligent species. This species, ironically, is a synthetic human creation.

In the first wave of AI, nearly 50 percent jobs are expected to go to machines. New technologies threaten about 40 percent of jobs in the United States and approximately two-thirds of those in the developing world (Gershon 2017).

The executive priorities will quickly shift. The pressure from shareholders to automate will take precedence.

Many of the factors from which traditional change theories were based upon – such as disconfirmation, increasing survival anxiety, creation of survival anxiety, cognitive redefinition, imitation, trial-and-error handling, and refreezing (Schein 1996) – will become irrelevant.

Eventually, companies may become self-managed operations. Many examples of such a transition are in the works and have implications on diverse industries and in several aspects in our lives. For example, a California-based pizza store (Zume) is now operated by robots. A hotel in Japan is almost entirely run by robots. Intuition Robotics, an Israeli firm that makes robots, acquired funding to develop a social companion robot called ElliQ to assist senior citizens living alone who are often isolated and lonely (McFarland 2017c). Pediatrician Dr. Harvey Karp, Yves Behar, and MIT-trained engineers created a bassinet (almost a robotic crib) called Snoo that comforts newborns through white noise, movement, and sensation of being swaddled (Kelly 2017). Poncho, a bot, was created to provide funny weather updates (Baraniuk 2017). Amazon launched Echo Look, a voice- and camera-driven AI assistant that helps customers dress better (Lopez 2017). Roboticists at the University of California, Berkeley, have developed a robot that can fold clothes (Gray 2017). Chatbots are emerging everywhere, allowing companies to establish automated chat programs in their platforms as an avenue to provide customer service (Baraniuk 2017). The field of telerobotics is emerging, where robots controlled by remote intelligence can be operated by a human manipulating its activity from a distance (Baldwin 2017). Robots are active in financial markets as traders and financial analysts.

In such a technology-dominant environment, an important question arises: How can leaders provide an organizational framework that can truly enable a better understanding of change?

Effective AI leadership require an altered perspective in how change is viewed. A new viewpoint is essential in five areas:

## *1. Evidence-Based Decision-Making*

Leaders must become accustomed to evidence-based decision-making. However, a leader must know what data was used to collect the evidence, its integrity and quality, and the process employed for evidence collection.

## *2. Complex System*

Leaders may need to develop an alternative perspective of their business. Instead of viewing it as a linear value chain, they may start seeing it as a complex system made up of many interdependent agents that transact with each other. This system can take many interesting shapes and evolve to new and previously unknown states.

## *3. Deviation from Human-Driven Explanations*

Human driven explanations can be biased. Using unbiased data and properly trained algorithms can help provide better explanations.

## *4. Use of Unstructured Data*

AI leaders can now use the unstructured data for both business and change management.

## *5. Development of Change Measurements*

Finally, measuring the rate of change itself can provide an important metric. This can be viewed as vectors that look at both the magnitude and direction of change.

A PWC (2016) report that pointed out several barriers the field of AI has to overcome concerns over data protection and privacy, consumer trust and regulatory acceptance, building relevant technologies, managing the volume of unstructured data, optimizing supply chain and production systems, and overcoming potentially high investment. Computers cannot simulate empathy and can't compete with human beings in understanding and connecting with other humans (Gershon 2017). Paul Gibbins, cofounder of chatbot start-up Twyla, indicated that script conversations can be challenging due to contextual communication differences (Baraniuk 2017). Furthermore, AI is not always the right solution (Popomaronis 2017), and only about 20 percent of the organizations possess essential skills to succeed with AI technology (Rao 2017). Given this multitude of challenges, dynamic and innovative business models have to be created effectively and in a rapid manner.

Strategic AI leadership approaches that can be helpful in this process include the following: (a) assessing opportunities and weighing in technology, competitive pressures and pain points, (b) determining key priorities, (c) ensuring resources relating to talent, culture and technology are in place, and (d) planning for proper governance and control with trust and transparency in mind (PWC 2016). Additionally, converging AI and ethics is critical in the future (Lufkin 2017).

## AI LEADERSHIP AND GOVERNANCE

Jim Leach, an academic and former member of the US House of Representatives, once said, "America somehow thinks that leadership relates to governance, and it certainly does. But society is much bigger than governance, and some of the truly great leadership of our society is outside the governance arena."

AI leaders need to think about the rationale for governance and what it constitutes. As the AI revolution brings about change, new platforms for management, power dynamics, authority, and control have to be assessed.

The market for AI remains small at about $644 million in 2016, but it is expected to increase to $15 billion by 2022 (Rao 2017). AI will contribute an estimated $15.7 trillion to the global economy by 2030 (PWC 2016). Start-ups have received billions in AI investments worldwide.

Researchers are burdened with demands placed upon them to understand, analyze, and examine various aspects of AI. For example, concerns remain in ethics (Abney 2011; Lin et al. 2012); in privacy (Calo 2011); in social interactions, including sex and love (Whitby 2012); and discrimination (Dwork and Hardt 2011).

Several cases of discrimination, manipulation, racism, privacy invasion, epistemic oppression, abuse, and exploitation have already been tied to AI. Autonomous technologies or AI-based artifacts have these salient features that makes them particularly vulnerable to be used for wicked purposes:

1. Ability to Make Complex Decisions: Autonomous systems can independently make complex decisions and display human-like decision-making characteristics, such as inference-based decision-making and heuristic decision-making, based upon very limited information.
2. Ability to Act in Wide Motion Spectrum: Modern robots can function as autonomous agents with higher degrees of freedom and display dexterity that was previously never present in synthetic systems.
3. Ability to Understand, Reason, and Strategize: Autonomous agents can reason, and can develop strategies in response to data.
4. Ability to Learn: Autonomous agents can learn from multiple sources including humans, their environment, and other autonomous agents.

Ability to Evolve: Autonomous agents can accumulate experience and evolve. This means that via new learning they can develop enhancements that allow them to perform activities that were beyond the scope or goals assigned to them or expected of them at the time of their creation.

The empowerment of AI in unprecedented levels requires a fresh approach on how we think and implement governance.

Governing intelligent and autonomous agents is one side of the problem. The other side is to manage and govern their impact on society, economy, and institution. Frey and Osborne (2013) estimated that AI has the potential to replace nearly 50 percent of all human jobs in the near term. Others also provide similar scenarios of job losses (Autor and Dorn 2013; Goos and Manning 2007). Unemployment of that scale can lead to an economic catastrophe.

The analysis presented in the last paragraph only focus on the labor replacement factor of AI and its consequences. This does not include the impact the autonomous agents can have on financial markets, economic activity, and wealth consolidation.

The next concerning stage of autonomous agents can be when they are intentionally deployed for the destructive or illegal purposes. This is where a human willfully unleashes an intelligent agent to conduct an illegal or destructive act. In 2017, 116 founders of robotics and AI companies called on the UN to ban autonomous weapons through an open letter. Elon Musk of Tesla and SpaceX was one of the signatories (Pham 2017). Musk believes that

AI is a higher risk than North Korea and if unchecked can lead to the death of humanity (Wattles 2017a).

The most troubling stage is when the autonomous agent can independently go bad and conduct illegal or destructive activities. This scenario is not too far-flung. Security robots are already in use and can be hazardous. There were instances where a security robot knocked over a child and was toppled over by a drunken man (Coleman 2017). A team of hackers doing a live stint in a Las Vegas stage was able to crack a Sentry Safe in 30 minutes using a $200 robot (Lee 2017).

AI has developed a four-step governance model. AI leaders need to weigh upon a governance framework through the assessment of four key areas:

1. AI Artifact Governance: The first step of governance is to understand and govern the ontological, ontic, and epistemological features of the technology itself. In this case, governance focuses on the artifact, its data, algorithms, and construction.
2. Owner, User, Distributor, and Developer Governance: The second level of governance focuses on humans involved in the development, design, marketing, conceptualizing, and use of the artifact.
3. Legal and Regulatory: This part governs the assessment that the technology meets the existing legal and regulatory requirements.
4. Human Impact Assessment: This part assesses the artifacts impact on human civilization including political, economic, social, moral, ethical, epistemic, psychological, and spiritual aspects of human life.

As the Figure 8.2 shows AI technology ecosystem includes many stakeholders. In many cases they form interdependent and symbiotic relationships. It is critical that governance and high ethical standards should be applied and practiced by all stakeholders.

The global community will be impacted by AI in profound ways. A PWC (2016) report indicated that countries projected to have the highest AI gains are China (26 percent GDP boost) and North America (14.5 percent GDP boost) consisting a total of 70 percent of the estimated $10.7 trillion global economic impact. Global trade will be positively impacted by AI since it (a) enables supply chains, (b) creates efficiency in compliance software, (c) speeds up and creates better trade contracts, and (d) improves access to finance (Nesbitt 2017). Due to its impact on product variety, personalization, attractiveness, and cost benefits, AI will contribute to 45 percent of all economic gains by 2030 (PWC 2016). Given the changes that are taking place, there are a multitude of influences as well as evolving factors to consider in the context of governance, organizations will be well served by assessing all options strategically.

Mehr (2017) identified the need for governments to (a) incorporate AI in their goals, (b) engage the citizenry, (c) build on existing resources, (d) consider data preparation, (e) manage ethical risks, and (f) strengthen employee potential. Some countries have started to pursue proactive measures. Singapore is aiming to be a pioneer as a Smart Nation where technology is merged with the way of life of all residents (Vaswani 2017).

In the coming years, companies and countries would be plotting out and executing the best governance strategies to gain new competitive advantages.

In this landscape, we would like to ask a few questions for AI leaders to think about: Do you want your medical devices, investment advisory software, and home robots to abide by ethics? Do you want your children to feel safe when they ride in an autonomous car? Do you want your personal and business systems to be protected from cyberattacks? Do you expect that you will not be exploited or manipulated as a customer?

If you answered yes to one or more of the above questions, you are asking for some type of governance. Governance is not regulation. It can exist on a purely volunteer basis.

Fearmongering is also not governance. But neither is denial or intentional ignorance.

We believe that just as denying the promise of progress associated with AI will be a travesty for the human civilization, unleashing technology without governance can lead to disastrous consequences.

In an expeditious manner, AI leaders need to start thinking about and implementing new governance models and operational frameworks.

## SADAL FRAMEWORK

A model proposed by the American Institute of Artificial Intelligence, SADAL (pronounced Saddle) framework, provides a good way to develop opportunities for AI automation. The process starts by looking at current business processes and then breaking them down into five parts: Sense, Analyze, Decide, Act, and Learn. As we have already observed that processes can be both mechanical and cognitive, the model applies to both.

# AI Leadership and the Way Forward

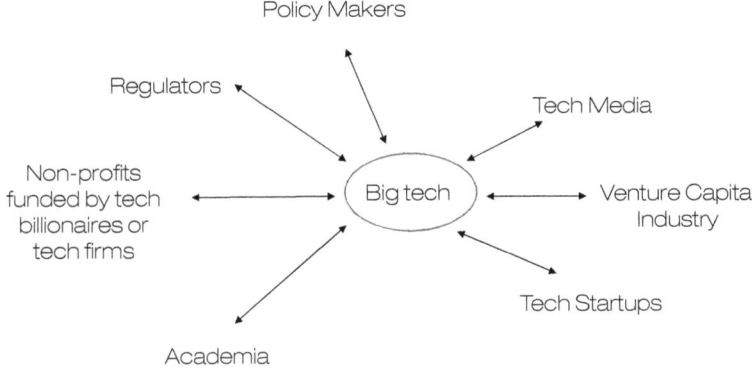

Symbiotic relationships that may need greater scrutiny for ethics and governance

**Figure 8.2.** AI stakeholder relationships

Sense: It means the mechanism by which an AI artifact uses sensors to receive or acquire information or data from its environment. In some ways, it is like human using their senses to see, hear, smell, touch, and taste.

Analyze: In this stage AI artifact processes the data to make it usable for its internal functioning.

Decide: Here the AI artifact makes decisions about its tasks.

Act: Based upon one or more decisions, the AI artifact takes actions that create a change in its environment.

Learn: The AI artifact learns from all four previous stages and become smarter. Based upon the new learning, it can adapt, evolve, and even change its goals.

Take the example of a radiology bot:

SENSE: Radiology bot receives images.
ANALYZE: Based upon existing state of learning, it can perform diagnostic analysis.
DECIDE: It can decide to make a recommendation to the physician—or when approved by the regulatory agencies, to the patient directly.
ACT: Based upon the results the bot can suggest diagnosis and provide clinical interventions.

Learn: The radiology bot can learn and improve not only from performing its core function but also learning about the patients.

The SADAL model is deployed to conceptualize products. AI will set the stage for productivity enhancement, economic transformation, and disruption and will be the foundation for new competitive advantages (PWC 2016). The SADAL model is the platform from which this takes place. For instance, in an effort to enhance guest experience and provide convenience and delight to customers, M Social Hotel in Singapore, a lifestyle hotel designed for millennial business travelers, created Aura, a room-service robot. Aura is the first of its kind outside of the United States and was created by robot-builders Savioke. Aura delivers bottled water and towels to rooms (Street 2017). ElliQ, a social companion robot designed for seniors, assists in communication with family, facilitates technology uses, gives out reminders such as doctor's appointments, and offers leisure suggestions such as walking or listening to music (McFarland 2017c). AI is predicted to be driving trucks by 2027, writing best-selling novels by 2049, and replacing surgeons by 2053 (Gray 2017).

## COGNITIVE MANAGEMENT

We recommend a 10-step plan for AI leaders to best manage their organizations in a cognitive era:

1. Educate yourself on the dynamics of competition in the cognitive era.
2. Decide on renewal. Make an executive decision to reinvent and redefine yourself.
3. Understand that this journey means building dual competencies in both your native core competencies and bot building.
4. Lead the cultural transformation to create unparalleled innovation.
5. Organize a cross-functional team to launch a major effort.
6. Analyze processes for what can be automated—both on physical and cognitive sides.
7. Apply the SADAL framework to each process. This implies that we need to determine the "what and how" of sensors, analytical, decision-making, action, and learning capabilities for the artifact you are building.
8. Making mistakes is an essential part of learning. The only way to build a good AI is to experiment, learn, and persevere.

9. Understand and have your boards and employees understand that competition is now about "cognitive competition."
10. Create an internal measure of cognitive competition map and constantly benchmark yourself against competitors.

## CONCLUSION

In the last scene of the movie *The Martian*, Mark Watney offers a powerful advice to the trainee astronauts: "You just do the math and solve the problem. And then onto the next problem and solve that problem. And solve the next problem too. And if you solve enough problems, you get to go home."

Bobby Unser, an American former automobile racer, once said, "Success is where preparation and opportunity meet." AI leaders who persevere and diligently plan and persevere through strategic cognition will likely reap the rewards.

AI and robotics will define and redefine the workplace in the coming years. As Sanjoe Jose mentioned in the chapter interview, "AI is not going to replace humans, but augment human capabilities to be superhumans."

We hope this book inspires corporate leaders to take on a new perspective on technology and what it means to humanity. We are living in interesting times, where leaders need mastery in the management of humans and machines.

Every day, there are multitudes of AI leaders furthering their business in different shapes and forms. Some are taking baby steps, others are making leaps and bounds. Investors are aggressively marshalling resources to support the industry. Governments are setting policies to promote and grow AI.

The world is in motion and has taken a concerted effort to take the AI revolution to highest heights. Similar to taking on a quest of Mt. Everest, humanity is stepping into an uncharted territory with elevated risks and opportunities for glory. Like the bold and knowledgeable Sherpas of Mt. Everest, AI leaders have the opportunity to serve as guides and mentors and lead the path toward a successful and amazing journey.

# REFERENCES

Abney, K. (2011). "Robotics, Ethical Theory, and Metaethics: A Guide for the Perplexed." In *Robot Ethics: The Ethical and Social Implications of Robotics*, ed. Patrick Lin, Keith Abney, and George A. Bekey, 35–52. Cambridge: MIT Press.

Arnoldi, J. (2015). "Computer Algorithms, Market Manipulation and the Institutionalization of High Frequency Trading." *Theory Culture & Society* 33 (1), 29–52.

Autor, D. H., and Dorn, D. (2013). "The Growth of Low Skill Service Jobs and the Polarization of the U. S. Labor Market." *American Economic Review* 103 (5), 1553–97.

Baldwin, R. (2017). "Forget AI. 'Remote Intelligence' Will Be Much More Disruptive." HuffPost. Accessed September 12, 2020. Available at: http://www.huffingtonpost.com/entry/telerobotics_us_5873bb48e4b02b5f858a1579.

Baraniuk, C. (2017). "Could Robots Put an End to Maddening Customer Service Calls?" BBC. Accessed September 14, 2020. Available at: http://www.bbc.com/capital/story/20170706-could-robots-put-an-end-to-maddening-customer-service-calls.

Bertocci, D. I. (2009). *Leadership in Organizations: There Is a Difference Between Leaders and Managers*. Lanham, MD: University Press of America.

Calo, M. R. (2011). "Robots and Privacy." In *Robot Ethics: The Ethical and Social Implications of Robotics*, ed. Patrick Lin, Keith Abney, and George A. Bekey. 187–202. Cambridge: MIT Press. Available from: https://www.google.com/books?hl=en&lr=&id=oBb-lt3l4oYC&oi=fnd&pg=PA187&dq=Robotics+and+the+Lessons+of+Cyberlaw+++Ryan+Calo+&ots=yudRw6BY_h&sig=bN_6v9fDLTXGhe-0BHn_8WUqbD0\nhttps://books.google.bg/books?hl=en&lr=&id=oBb-lt3l4oYC&oi=fnd&pg=PA187&dq=Robotics.

Carmeli, A., and Schaubroeck, J. (2008). "Organisational Crisis-Preparedness: The Importance of Learning from Failures." *Long Range Planning* 41 (2), 177–96.

Coleman, N. (2017). "Security Robot 'In Critical Condition' after Nearly Drowning on the Job." CNN. Accessed September 18, 2020. Available at: http://www.cnn.com/2017/07/18/us/security-robot-drown-trnd/?iid=ob_homepage_deskrecommended_pool.

Collier, A. T. (1978). *Business Leadership and a Creative Society*. Cambridge: Harvard Business Review, 1968.

Domingos, P. (2015). *The Master Algorithm: How the Quest for the Ultimate Learning Machine Will Remake Our World*. New York: Basic Books. Kindle Edition.

Dowd, M. (2017). "Elon Musk's Billion-Dollar Crusade to Stop the A.I. Apocalypse." *Vanity Fair*. Accessed April 8, 2020. Available at: https://www.vanityfair.com/news/2017/03/elon-musk-billion-dollar-crusade-to-stop-ai-space-x.

Dunbar, K. (1998). "Problem Solving." In *A Companion to Cognitive Science*, ed. W. Bechtel and G. Graham, 289–98. London: Blackwell.

Dwork, C., and Hardt, M. (2011). Fairness through Awareness. arXiv.org. Accessed Feb 12, 2021. Available at: https://arxiv.org/pdf/1104.3913.pdf.

Edwards, G., Schedlitzki, D., Turnbull, S., and Gill, R. (2015). "Exploring Power Assumptions in the Leadership and Management Debate." *Leadership & Organization Development Journal* 36 (3), 328–43.

Eisenberg, E. M., Johnson, Z., and Pieterson, W. (2015). "Leveraging Social Networks for Strategic Success." *International Journal of Business Communication* 52 (521), 143–54.

Ferris, R. (2016). "Machines Have a Serious Advantage over Human Investors." CNBC. Wednesday, June 29. Available at: http://www.cnbc.com/2016/06/29/machines-have-a-serious-advantage-over-human-investors.html.

Financial Times (2018). "John Deere Ploughs a New Furrow with Algorithmic Acquisition." Accessed April 5, 2020. Available at: https://www.ft.com/content/3c7c84c4-94f3-11e7-a9e6-11d2f0ebb7f0.

Fleming, P., and Spicer, A. (2003). "Working at a Cynical Distance: Implications for Power, Subjectivity and Resistance." *Organization* 10 (1), 157–79.

Frey C. B., and Osborne M. A. (2013). "The Future of Employment: How Susceptible Are Jobs to Computerisation?" Oxford: Oxford University Press. Available at: http://www.oxfordmartin.ox.ac.uk/downloads/academic/The_Future_of_Employment.pdf.

Gast, A., and Lansink, R. (2015). "Digital Hives: Creating a Surge Around Change." *Mckinsey Quarterly* 2, 1–9.

Gershon, L. (2017). "The Automation Resistant Skills We Should Nurture." BBC. Accessed September 9, 2020. Available at: http://www.bbc.com/capital/story/20170726-the-automation-resistant-skills-we-should-nurture.

Gillespie, P. (2017). "Rise of the Machines: Fear Robots Not China or Mexico." Accessed April 11, 2020. Available at: http://money.cnn.com/2017/01/30/news/economy/jobs-china-mexico-automation/index.html.

Gladwell, M. (2005). *Blink: The Power of Thinking without Thinking*. New York: Little, Brown, 155–66.

Gluck, F. (1980). "Strategic Choices and Research Allocation." *McKinsey Quarterly* 1, 22–33.

Goos, M., and Manning, A. (2007). "Lousy and Lovely Jobs: The Rising Polarization of Work in Britain." *Review of Economics and Statistics* 89 (1), 118–33. Available at: http://econpapers.repec.org/RePEc:tpr:restat:v:89:y:2007:i:1:p:118-133.

Gray, R. (2017). "How Long Will It Take for Your Job to Be Automated?" BBC. Accessed September 13, 2020. Available at: http://www.bbc.com/capital/story/20170619-how-long-will-it-take-for-your-job-to-be-automated.

Grint, K. (2005). "Problems, Problems, Problems: The Social Construction of 'Leadership.'" *Human Relations* 58 (11), 1467–94.

Holley, P. (2015). "Bill Gates on Dangers of Artificial Intelligence: I Don't Understand Why Some People Are Not Concerned." Accessed April 2, 2020. Available at: https://www.washingtonpost.com/news/the-switch/wp/2015/01/28/bill-gates-on-dangers-of-artificial-intelligence-dont-understand-why-some-people-are-not-concerned/?utm_term=.193c108e683c.

Isabella, L. A. (1990). Evolving Interpretations as a Change Unfolds: How Managers Construe Key Organizational Events." *Academy of Management Journal* 33 (1), 7–41.

Kelly, S. M. (2017). "A Robotic Crib Rocked My Baby to Sleep for Months." CNN Tech. Accessed September 20, 2020. Available at: http://money.cnn.com/2017/08/10/technology/gadgets/snoo-review/index.html?iid=ob_homepage_tech_pool.

Kilborn, P. (2001). "An Illinois Tire Plant Closes and a Way of Life Fades." Accessed April 8, 2020. Available at: http://www.nytimes.com/2001/12/14/us/an-illinois-tire-plant-closes-and-a-way-of-life-fades.html.

Landry, M. (1995). "A Note on the Concept of 'Problem' Organization Studies." *Organization Studies* 16 (2), 315–43.

LeBaron, D. (2010). "The Inevitable Baggage We Display." *Journal of Investment Management* 8 (2), 5–8. Available at: http://www.deanlebaron.com/JOIM_2010_final.pdf.

Lee, D. (2017). "Robot Cracks Open Safe Live on Def Con's Stage." BBC. Accessed September 05, 2020. Available at: http://www.bbc.com/news/technology-40760648.

Lewis, P. J. (1992). "Rich Picture Building in the Soft Systems Methodology." *European Journal of Information Systems* 1 (5), 351–60. Available at: http://www.palgrave-journals.com/ejis/journal/v1/n5/abs/ejis19927a.html.

Lin, P., Abney, K., and Bekey, G. A. (2012). "Roboethics: The Applied Ethics for a New Science," in *Robot Ethics: The Ethical and Social Implications of Robotics,* ed. Patrick Lin, Keith Abney, and George A. Bekey, 347–63. Cambridge: MIT Press.

Lopez, N. (2017). "Amazon Unveils Echo Look, a $199 AI Assistant That Gives You Fashion Tips." TNW. Accessed September 26, 2020. Available at: https://thenextweb.com/gadgets/2017/04/26/amazon-unveils-echo-look-199-ai-assistant-gives-fashion-tips/#.tnw_SCOzaUdN.

Lufkin, B. (2017). "Why the Biggest Challenge Facing AI Is an Ethical One." BBC. Accessed September 26, 2020. Available at: http://www.bbc.com/future/story/20170307-the-ethical-challenge-facing-artificial-intelligence.

McDonald, F. (2015). "A Robot Just Passed a Classic Self-Awareness Test for the First Time." Accessed April 8, 2018. Available at: http://www.sciencealert.com/a-robot-has-just-passed-a-classic-self-awareness-test-for-the-first-time.

McFarland, M. (2017a). "Popular YouTube Artist Uses AI to Record New Album." CNN Tech. Accessed September 20, 2020. Available at: http://money.cnn.com/2017/08/21/technology/future/taryn-southern-ai-music/index.html?iid=ob_homepage_tech_pool.

———. (2017b). "Farmers Turn to Artificial Intelligence to Grow Better Crops." CNN Tech. Accessed September 20, 2020. Available at: http://money.cnn.com/2017/07/26/technology/future/farming-ai-tomatoes/index.html.

———. (2017c). "Can Robots Solve Grandma's Loneliness?" CNN Tech. Accessed September 20, 2020. Available at: http://money.cnn.com/2017/07/11/technology/culture/robot-senior-citizen/index.html?iid=ob_homepage_deskrecommended_pool.

Mehr, H. (2017). "Artificial Intelligence: 6 Steps Government Agencies Can Take." *State Scoop.* Accessed September 20, 2020. Available at: http://statescoop.com/artificial-intelligence-6-steps-government-agencies-can-take.

McKinsey (2018). "Advanced Electronics." Accessed April 15, 2020. Available at: https://www.mckinsey.com/industries/advanced-electronics/our-insights/artificial-intelligence-the-time-to-act-is-now.

Miller, Claire Cain (2016). "The Real Long-Term Jobs Killer Is Not China. It's Automation. New York Times, December 21. Accessed September 2018. Available at: https://www.nytimes.com/2016/12/21/upshot/the-long-term-jobs-killer-is-not-china-its-automation.html.

Miyazaki, A. D., and Taylor, K. A. (2008). "Researcher Interaction Biases and Business Ethics Research: Respondent Reactions to Researcher Characteristics." *Journal of Business Ethics* 81 (4), 779–95.

Morrison, E. W., and Milliken, F. J. (2000). "Organizational Silence: A Barrier to Change and Development in a Pluralistic World." *Academy of Management Review* 25 (4), 706–25. Available at: http://amr.aom.org/cgi/doi/10.5465/AMR.2000.3707697.

Murgia, M. (May 24, 2016). "Humans vs. Robots: Meet the World Champion Who Lost to Google's Two-Year-Old Computer Program." Accessed March 21, 2020. Available at: http://s.telegraph.co.uk/graphics/projects/go-google-computer-game/.

Nesbitt, J. (2017). "4 Ways Artificial Intelligence Is Transforming Trade." *Trade Ready*. Accessed September 25, 2020. Available at: http://www.tradeready.ca/2017/topics/import-export-trade-management/4-ways-artificial-intelligence-transforming-trade/.

New World AI (2019). "The Coming Singularity: Ray Kurzweil." Accessed September 2, 2020. Available at: https://www.newworldai.com/the-coming-singularity-ray-kurzweil/.

Newell, A., and Simon, H. A. (1972). *Human Problem Solving*. Englewood Cliffs, NJ: Prentice-Hall.

Pearson, C. M., and Clair, J. A. (1998). "Reframing Crisis Management." *Academy of Management Review* 23 (1), 59–76.

PBS (2013). "Obama Calls for Long-Term Economic Plan to Help Middle Class Rebound." Accessed April 5, 2020. Available at: http://www.pbs.org/newshour/bb/politics-july-dec13-obama_07-24/.

Pham, S. (2017). "Elon Musk Backs Call for Global Ban on Killer Robots." CNN Tech. Accessed September 16, 2020. Available at: http://money.cnn.com/2017/08/21/technology/elon-musk-killer-robot-un-ban/index.html.

Piderit, S. K. (2000). "Rethinking Resistance and Recognizing Ambivalence: A Multidimensonal View of Attitudes toward an Organizational Change." *Academy of Management Review* 25 (4), 783. Available at: http://www.emeraldinsight.com.ezp.waldenulibrary.org/loi/jocm%5Cnhttp://karhen.home.xs4all.nl/Papers/M&A/Piderit (2000).pdf.

Popomaronis, T. (2017). "11 Tech Leaders Share the Real Truth about Artificial Intelligence (and What Really Matters)." Accessed September 2, 2020. Available at: https://www.forbes.com/sites/tompopomaronis/2017/08/29/11-tech-leaders-share-insights-on-artificial-intelligence-and-what-actually-matters/#2c7c758e6668.

PWC (2016). "Sizing the Prize. PWC's Global Artificial Intelligence Study: Exploiting the AI Revolution." Accessed September 2, 2020. Available at: https://www.pwc.com/gx/en/issues/data-and-analytics/publications/artificial-intelligence-study.html.

Quoteinvestigator (2018). "Quotes." Accessed April 8, 2019. Available at: https://quoteinvestigator.com/category/anne-isabella-thackeray-ritchie/#note-11878-1.

Raelin, J. A. (2003). *Creating Leaderful Organizations: How to Bring Out Leadership in Everyone*. San Francisco, CA: Berrett-Koehler.

Rao, A. (2017). "A Strategist's Guide to Artificial Intelligence. Strategy + Business." Accessed September 4, 2020. Available at: https://www.strategy-business.com/article/A-Strategists-Guide-to-Artificial-Intelligence?gko=0abb5&utm_source=itw&utm_medium=20170523&utm_campaign=respB.

Rawlings, N. (2013). "Why Obama Keeps Going Back to One Small Illinois College." *Time*. Accessed April 9, 2020. Available at: http://nation.time.com/2013/07/24/why-obama-keeps-going-back-to-one-small-illinois-college/.

Reynolds, N. (2015). "Making Sense of New Technology during Organisational Change." *New Technology, Work and Employment* 30 (2), 145–57.

Rossi, B. (2017). "How Tesco Is Using AI to Gain Customer Insight." Accessed April 9, 2020. Available at: http://www.information-age.com/tesco-using-ai-gain-customer-insight-123466328/.

Rost, J. C. (1993). *Leadership for the Twenty-First Century*. New York: Praeger.

Samuelson, P., and Mankiw, N. G. (2009). "Is Government Spending Too Easy an Answer?" *New York Times*, January 10. Accessed May 4, 2020. Available at: http://www.nytimes.com/2009/01/11/business/economy/11view.html?_r=0.

Schein, E. H. (1996). "Kurt Lewin's Change Theory in the Field and in the Classroom: Notes toward a Model of Managed Learning." *Systems Practice* 9 (1), 27–47.

Shane, Scott, and Wakabayashi, Daisuke (2018). "'The Business of War': Google Employees Protest Work for the Pentagon." *New York Times*. Accessed June 25, 2020. Available at: https://www.nytimes.com/2018/04/04/technology/google-letter-ceo-pentagon-project.html.

Silver, D., Schrittwieser, J., Simonyan, K., et al. (2017). "Mastering the Game of Go without Human Knowledge." *Nature* 550, 354–59. Available at: https://doi.org/10.1038/nature24270.

Street, F. (2017). "Introducing AURA, the Room Service Robot." CNN. Accessed September 4, 2020. Available at: http://www.cnn.com/travel/article/singapore-room-service-robot-aura/index.html.

Surmacz, D. (2017). "AI Recommendations That Know You Better Than You Know Yourself." Accessed April 4, 2020. Available at: http://digitalmarketingmagazine.co.uk/digital-marketing-features/ai-recommendations-that-know-you-better-than-you-know-yourself.

Taleb, N. N. ([2007] 2010). *The Black Swan: The Impact of the Highly Improbable* (2nd edn.). London: Penguin. ISBN 978-0-14103459-1.

Turner, B. A. (1976). "The Organizational and Interorganizational Development of Disasters." *Administrative Science Quarterly* 21 (3), 378–97.

Vaswani, K. (2017). "Tomorrow's Cities: Singapore's Plans for a Smart Nation." BBC. Accessed September 2, 2020. Available at: http://www.bbc.com/news/technology-39641262.

Vince, R., Broussine, M. (1996). "Paradox, Defense and Attachment: Accessing and Working with Emotions and Relations Underlying Organizational Change." *Organizational Studies* 17, 11–21.

Wattles, J. (2017a). "A Bot Just Defeated One of the World's Best Videogamers." CNN Tech. Accessed September 2, 2020. Available at: http://money.cnn.com/2017/08/12/technology/future/elon-musk-ai-dota-2/index.html.

———. (2017b). "Robot Makes Money Off Trump's Tweets and Donates it to ASPCA." CNN. Accessed September 2, 2020. Available at: http://money.cnn.com/2017/02/06/technology/trump-dump-stock-short-selling/index.html?iid=ob_homepage_tech_pool.

Whitby, B. (2012). "Do You Want a Robot Lover? The Ethics of Caring Technologies." In *Robot Ethics: The Ethical and Social Implications of Robotics*, ed. Patrick Lin, Keith Abney, and George A. Bekey, 233–48. Cambridge: MIT Press.

Ezzamel, M., Worthington, F., and Willmot, H. (2001). "Power, Control and Resistance in 'the Factory That Time Forgot.'" *Journal of Management Studies* 38 (8), 1053–79. Available at: http://onlinelibrary.wiley.com/doi/10.1111/1467-6486.00272/abstract.

# INDEX

Adams, Jeff
   on AI opportunities 2–3
   on automation 3
   on current state of AI, 1
   on effect of AI, 1–2
   on future of AI in workplace, 4
   on offences in AI revolution, 2
   on prioritization of AI projects, 3
   on stakeholders' role, 3–4
adaptability to change, 76
ADM, 123
agility, 23
agriculture tools, 18
AI agents, 130–31
AI change, 134–36
   and complex system, 136
   and development of change measurement, 136
   and evidence-based decision making, 136
   and human-driven explanations, 136
   and use of unstructured data, 136
AI circles, 78
AI governance, 129–34
AI steering committees, 78
algorithms, 29, 32, 39, 40–41, 134
AlphaGo, 9, 43
Amazon, 53, 135
Amper Music, 76
artificial neural networks, 41–42
art of winning (AI problem related story), 98–100
audit services, 128–29

Aura, 142
automation, 21–22, 126–27. *See also* intelligent automation
   cognitive automation, 14, 67
   cost of, 6–9
   develop automation, 44
   do automation, 44
   industrial automation, 133
   responsibility, 5
   robotic process automation, 43–44
   think automation, 44
autonomous weapons, 138

back propagation, 41
Basu, Arindom, 100
   on automation, 85
   best practices, 85
   on current state of AI, 83–84
   on effect of AI, 84
   on essential leadership attributes, 86
   on future of AI in workplace, 86
   on offences in AI revolution, 84–85
   on organizational challenges, 84
   on prioritization of AI projects, 85
   on stakeholders' role, 86
   on value creation by AI, 84
Bayesian networks, 41
Behar, Yves, 135
better than cocaine (AI problem related story), 96–98
bias, 19, 55–56
big data, 6, 15
Blue River Technology, 65

Boeing, 4, 76
Bostrom, Nick, 33
bots, 58, 130, 135
Bush, George W., 129–30
business context. *See* State 1 Leadership
business leadership, 60
business models, 66–67
business operations, assessment and optimization of, 77–78
business value creation, 127

caterpillar, 123
centralized planning model, 54–55
challenges for humankind, 125–26
change
    adaptability to, 76
    considerations for, 132
    measurement, development of, 136
    process, leading up to crisis events, 134
chatbots, 135
China, 9
Climate Basic, 129
Climate Corporation, 132
Clinton, Bill, 129
clustering, 41
cognitive automation, 14, 67
cognitive management, 142–43
cognitive revolution, 26
competition, 69
competitive assessment, 79
complex decision-making ability, of autonomous systems, 138
complex systems, 136
    self-evolving, 131
concerns, regarding AI, 136–39
connectivity, 28, 32
crop and soil health monitoring, 17–18

Danilo, Raphael
    on AI challenges, 34
    on AI opportunities, 35
    on automation, 35–36
    best practices, 36
    on current state of AI, 33
    on effect of AI, 33
    on essential leadership attributes, 37
    on future of AI in workplace, 37
    on offences in AI revolution, 34–35
    on prioritization of AI projects, 36
    on stakeholders' role, 36–37
    value creation by AI, 34
data, 28–29, 32, 40–41
data-centric decision-making, 56
data centric solution development, 131
data collection challenges, 20
data management, 29
Decatur, 123–24
decisions by machines, reliance on, 56–57
decision tree learning, 41
deep company, 9
deep learning, 41, 42
Deere, John, 65
Degnan, Oliver, 81
    on AI opportunities, 72
    on automation, 72
    best practices, 72
    on current state of AI, 71
    on effect of AI, 71
    on essential leadership attributes, 73
    on future of AI in workplace, 73
    on offences in AI revolution, 72
    on organizational challenges, 72
    on prioritization of AI projects, 72
    on stakeholders' role, 73
    on value creation by AI, 72
Deloitte, 128
destructive or illegal purposes, autonomous agents deployment, 138
digital workers, 10–11
Domingos, Pedro, 41
Driscoll's, 65

Echo Look, 135
economic impact, 139
economy, 14
education on AI and robotics, 76
effective leadership, 73–74
Einstein, Albert, 17
ElliQ (robot), 135, 142
e-mails, 39
emotional intelligence (EQ), 23
employee concerns, 132–33

# Index

employee skill sets, reviewing and revitalization, 78
ethics, 16, 51. *See also* State 2 Leadership
evidence-based decision-making, 136
evolving ability, of autonomous agents, 138
executive considerations, emerging, 75–76
EY, 128

factory worker (workplace scenario), 110–12
fake news, 15
farming, automation in, 21
finance, AI in, 74
financial considerations, 80
Firestone, 123
firm boundaries, 131
flywheel concept (Amazon), 53
forecast data, 17
Frey, C. B., 138
future of AI leadership, 120–27

Gates, Bill, 55, 130
generalization of things, 39
Gibbins, Paul, 137
globalization, 11
global trade, AI's impact on, 139
Go (game), human vs computer, 9–10
goal setting, 79
Google, 132–33
governance, and AI leadership, 137–40
governance model, 139
graphics processing units (GPUs), 42
Great Recession, 11–13, 125–26

Hawking, Stephen, 55, 130
health industry, automation in, 21
hospitals, AI in, 75–76
human civilization value creation, 127
human-driven explanations, 136
human interests, and commercial value, 127
human resources, AI in, 74
human species versus computer, 9–10
human versus computer Jeopardy competition, 24–25
humble confidence, 24

IBM, 24–25, 129
IBM Watson, 54
identity management, automation in, 22
impact of AI, 139–40
implementation of programs, 80
inductive logic programming, 41
industrial automation, 133
industrial revolution, fourth, 13, 26
industrial revolutions, 25–26, 64
infiltrators (AI problem related story), 94–96
influence, 59–60
information revolution, 26
information technology revolution, 11
infrastructure and technology, 79
innovation
  AI centric, 68
  and commercial value, 127
intelligent automation, 4, 5
  digital workers, 10–11
  disruptive power of, 8–9
  era of, 25–26
  winters of, 27–28
Internet, 26, 28
Internet of Things (IoT), 28
Internet revolution, 52
Intuition Robotics, 135
investor relations management, AI in, 74

Jeopardy (TV program), 24–25
job losses, due to automation and AI, 133, 135, 138
Jose, Sanjoe, 143
  on AI opportunities, 105
  on automation, 105
  best practices, 106
  on current state of AI, 103
  on effect of AI, 104
  on essential leadership attributes, 106
  on future of AI in workplace, 107
  on offences in AI revolution, 105
  on organizational challenges, 104
  on prioritization of AI projects, 105
  on stakeholders' role, 106
  on value creation by AI, 104
Josephson, Michael, 71

Karp, Harvey, 135
Kennedy, John F., 135
Khanna, Gaurav, 32
  on AI opportunities, 21
  on automation, 21–22
  best practices, 22
  on current state of AI, 17–18
  on effect of AI, 18–19
  on future of AI in workplace, 24
  on leadership attributes, 23–24
  on offences in AI revolution, 20
  on organizational challenges, 19–20
  on prioritization of AI projects, 22
  on stakeholders' role, 23
  on value creation by AI, 19
Knox College, 124–25
KPMG, 128
Kurzwell, Ray, 121

Laing, R. D., 1
language technology, 2
layoffs, 87
Leach, Jim, 137
leaders. *See also* State 1 Leadership; State 2 Leadership; State 3 Leadership
  responsibility of, 5
  self-awareness, 16
  traits, 5
leadership theories, 50
learning ability, of autonomous agents, 138
luminance, 129

MacArthur, Douglas, 103
machine learning (ML), 38
  automation via, 44
  types of, 39–40
managers, 58–59, 66
manpower, for AI development, 20
market assessment, 79
marketing, AI in, 74
market researcher (workplace scenario), 116–18
McKinsey, 88
Mehr, H., 140
Minsky, Marvin, 40

mission, 79
M Social Hotel, 142
multidimensional interaction, 131
Munoz, Mark, 80
Murgia, Madhumita, 9–10
Musk, Elon, 55, 77, 130, 138–39

Naqvi, Al, 75, 128
narrow AI, 26
NatureSweet, 64, 129
network capabilities, 28
neural networks, 41–42, 75
new personal leadership qualities development. *See* State 3 Leadership

Obama, Barack, 125
objective leadership, 57
Olsen, Ken, 88
Open AI, 77
organizational design and preparation, 80
organizational silence, 133
Orton, William, 88
Osborne, M. A., 138
Oscar W. Larson Company, 129

participation in AI and robotics initiatives, 76
perfect information, 35
pesticides usage, decrement in, 18
planning, 78
Platts, Chris, 60
  on AI opportunities, 48
  on automation, 48
  best practices, 49
  on challenges related to AI, 48
  on current state of AI, 47
  on effect of AI, 47
  on future of AI in workplace, 49
  on offences in AI revolution, 48
  on stakeholders' role, 49
  on value creation by AI, 48
Poncho (bot), 135
Powell, Jerome H., 14
Presidential Leadership Scholars Programs, 129–30

proactivity, 77–79
problem domains, 131
problems definition, 54
problems related to AI (stories)
   art of winning, 98–100
   better than cocaine, 96–98
   infiltrators, 94–96
   spy cab, 89–90
   travel planner, 90–91
   virtual recruiter, 92–94
processing and analytical capabilities, 28, 31–32
processing power, 32
product bias, 56
programming, 38
publisher (workplace scenario), 112–16
PWC, 128

quick learners, 24
quote-investigation, 37

reinforcement and deep learning, combined, 43
reinforcement learning, 40, 41
relationships and alliances, 80
Rensselaer Polytechnic Institute, 120–21
responsibility, and automation, 5
responsible adoption, 87–89
retail store cashier (workplace scenario), 107–10
review and evaluation, 80
risk assessment, 80
risks of AI, 55, 130
Rivet Model for AI leadership, 122–23, 124
robotic process automation (RPA), 43–44
robots, 135–36
   in factories, 67–68
   learning by, 40, 43

SADAL framework, 140–42
Samuelson, Paul, 7
Savioke, 142

searchable codified knowledge, 131
security robots, 139
Sedol, Lee, 9–10
self-awareness, and value creation, 57–58
self-evolving complex systems, 131
self-managed operations, 135
self-reflection, 131
Sharrett, Luke, 14
Silver, David, 43
simulation, 131
Singapore, 140
Sírio-Libanês Hospital, Brazil, 75
skills building, 76
Snoo (bassinet), 135
social media, 133
social sciences, and work, 30–31
social silence, 133
Southern, Taryn, 76
speech technology, 2
spy cab (AI problem related story), 89–90
stakeholders, 139
stakeholders engagement, 78
State 1 Leadership, 64–65
   AI-centric transformation programs, 53
   centralized planning model, 54
   challenge, 65–66
   competition, understanding of, 69
   defining the problems, 54
   definition, 51, 52
   development of new business models, 66–67
   development of new employee skill sets, 67–68
   innovation, 68
   integrating AI in strategic planning, 53
   internal and external environmental changes, 68–69
   knowing the difference between AI and IT, 53–54
   planning, 54
   responding to AI and robotics revolution, 69

State 2 Leadership, 73–75
  adaptability to change, 76
  bias removal, 55–56
  definition, 51, 55
  education and skills building, 76
  emerging executive
    considerations, 75–77
  innovation, 76
  internal and external environmental
    changes, 77
  learning about technology, 56
  participation in initiatives, 76
  proactivity, 77–79
  responding to AI and robotics
    revolution, 77
  understanding risks of AI, 55
State 3 Leadership, 86–87
  communication, 58
  definition, 51–52
  leadership style analysis by AI, 57
  management approaches, 58–59
  problems related to AI, 89–101
  reliance on decisions by
    machines, 56–57
  responsible adoption, 87–89
  self-awareness and value
    creation, 57–58
strategic AI leadership, 137
strategic bias, 56
strategic plan, 78–81
  financial considerations, 80
  implementation, 80
  infrastructure and technology, 79–80
  market and competitive assessment, 79
  mission and goals, 79
  operational assessment, 79
  organizational design and
    preparation, 80
  relationships and alliances, 80
  review and evaluation, 80
  risk assessment, 80
strategic planning, integrating AI in, 53
subjective leadership, 50
supervised learning, 40
supply chain management, AI in, 75
surgeon (workplace scenario), 118–20

T3, 77
Tate and Lyle, 123
teaching machines, 38–39. *See also*
  machine learning (ML)
telerobotics, 135–36
Tracy, Brian, 61
transformation, leading of. *See* State 1
  Leadership
travel planner (AI problem related
  story), 90–91
Tripathi, Subhashini Sharma, 70
  on AI opportunities, 62
  on automation, 63
  best practices, 63
  on current state of AI, 61
  on effect of AI, 61–62
  on essential leadership attributes,
    63–64
  on future of AI in workplace, 64
  on offences in AI revolution, 62
  on organizational challenges, 62
  on prioritization of AI projects, 63
  on stakeholders' role, 63
  on value creation by AI, 62
Turner, B. A., 134
Twyla, 137

uncertainty, 66
understanding, reasoning, and
  strategization ability, of autonomous
  agents, 138
United States
  2016 presidential election, 6–8, 11–
    12, 15
  business planning and policy
    making in, 13
  fixing immigration problem with
    AI, 64–65
University of California, 135
Unser, Bobby, 143
unstructured data, use of, 136
unsupervised learning, 40

value creation, 127
virtual recruiter (AI problem related
  story), 92–94

Warren, Elizabeth, 89
Watson (smart computer), 25
wide motion spectrum, autonomous agents' ability to act in, 138
wise men puzzle, 120–21
Woodside Energy, 54
work, 29–31
workplace
   finance, 74
   human resources, 73–74
   investor relations management, 74
   marketing, 74
   supply chain management, 75
workplace scenarios
   factory worker, 110–12
   market researcher, 116–18
   publisher, 112–16
   retail store cashier, 107–10
   surgeon, 118–20

Zanuck, Darryl, 88
Zume, 135

www.ingramcontent.com/pod-product-compliance
Ingram Content Group UK Ltd.
Pitfield, Milton Keynes, MK11 3LW, UK
UKHW041140160426
5217IPUK00045B/32